TABLE OF CONTENT

This pattern is written in US Standard Crochet Terms, as assumes knowledge of basin stitches.

- rnd = Row/Round
- slst = Slip stitch

- ch = chain
- sc = single crochet
- hdc = half double crochet
- dc = double crochet

- tr = treble crochet

- mr = magic ring

- dc inc = crochet two double crochet into 1 stitch

- inc = sc increase (2sc into same stitch)
- dec = sc decrease (crochet 2sc together)
- *Tips: Use invisible decrease for better finished*
- tr = treble crochet
- FLO = front loop only
- BLO = Back loop only
- [.....]
- = When it begins a sentence, replicate the sequence enclosed within the square brackets as many times as indicated.
- = When it appears at the end of a sentence, such as [6], it signifies the total number of stitches required at the end of the row.
- hdc inc = crochet two half double crochet into 1 stitch
- dc inc = two double crochet into the same stitch

PART II: SEA CREATURES CROCHET PATTERN

2.1 Requirements

- **Skill level**

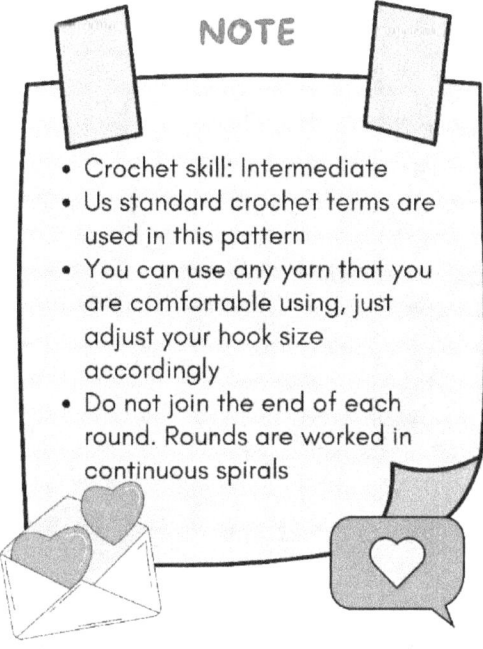

NOTE

- Crochet skill: Intermediate
- Us standard crochet terms are used in this pattern
- You can use any yarn that you are comfortable using, just adjust your hook size accordingly
- Do not join the end of each round. Rounds are worked in continuous spirals

- **Yarn** (You can use any type of yarn. Different yarn and hook will create different size of finished toy)

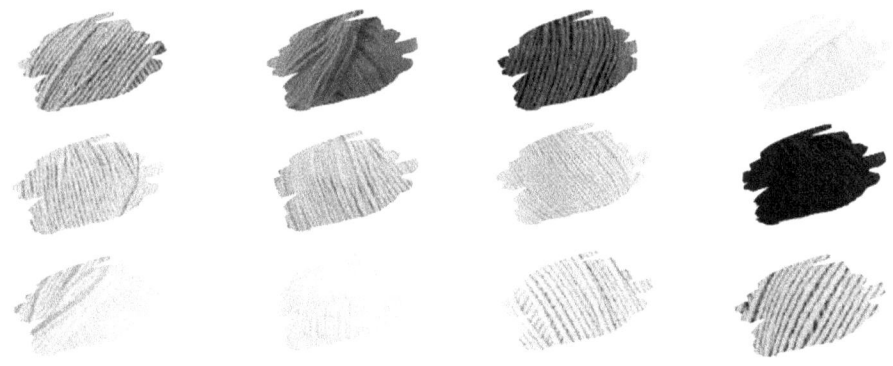

- **Accessories**

2.2 Octopus Crochet Pattern

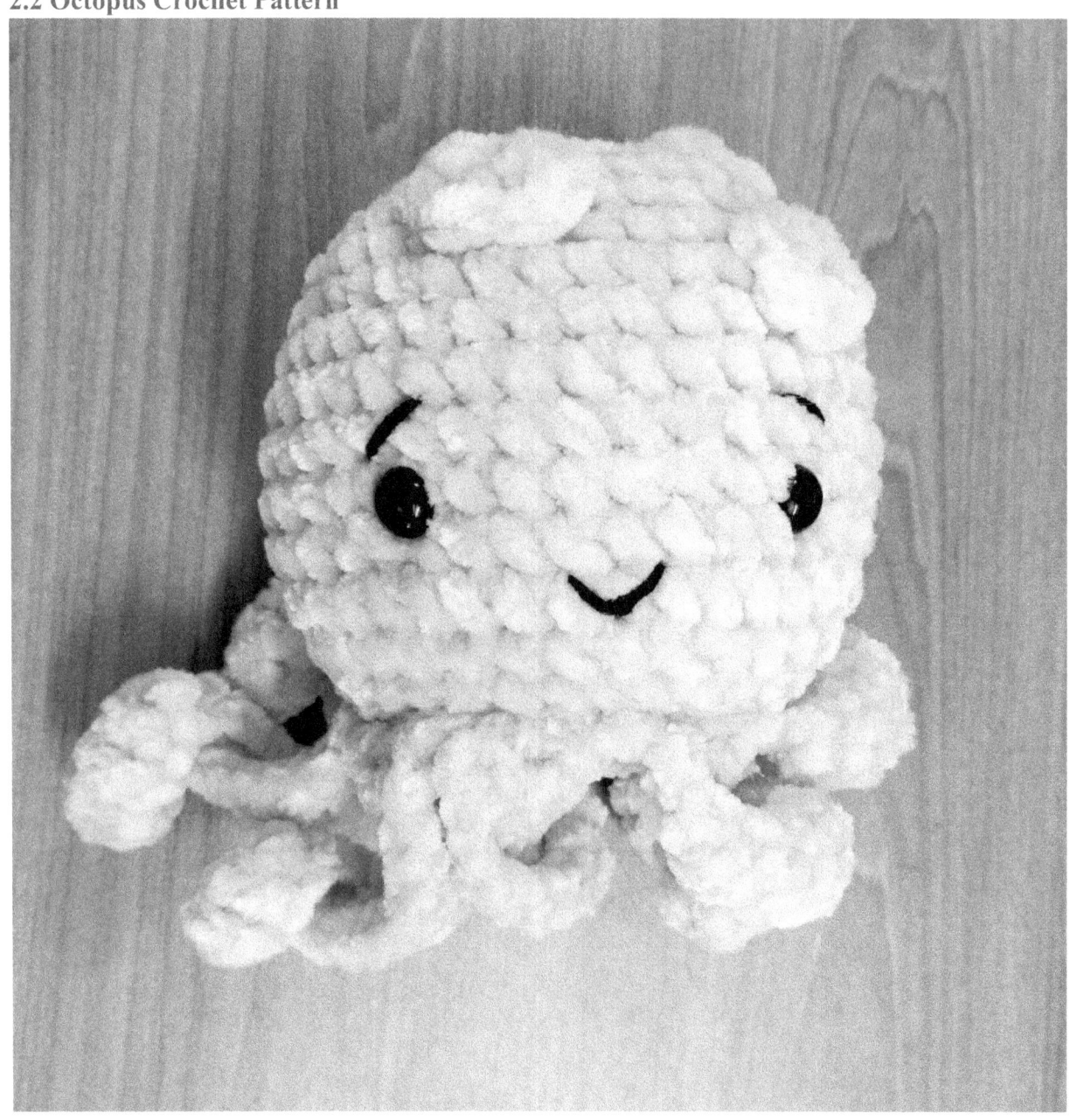

Head and Body

Start with Pink Yarn

Rnd 1: Make 8sc into MR [8]

Rnd 2: 8inc [16]

Rnd 3: (sc, inc) repeat 8 times [24]

Rnd 4: (2sc, inc) repeat 8 times [32]

Rnd 5: 32sc all around [32]

Rnd 6: (3sc, inc) repeat 8 times [40]

Rnd 7 – Rnd 13: 40sc all around – total 7 rounds [40]

Rnd 14: (3sc, dec) repeat 8 times [32]

Rnd 15: 32sc all around [32]

If you use safety eyes, insert the eyes between round 11 and 12 with 7 stitches apart.

Start stuffing the head firmly, adding more as you go.

Rnd 16: BLO all (2sc, dec) repeat 8 times [24]

Rnd 17: (sc, dec) repeat 8 times [16]

Rnd 18: 8dec [8]

Fasten off and wave the yarn tail

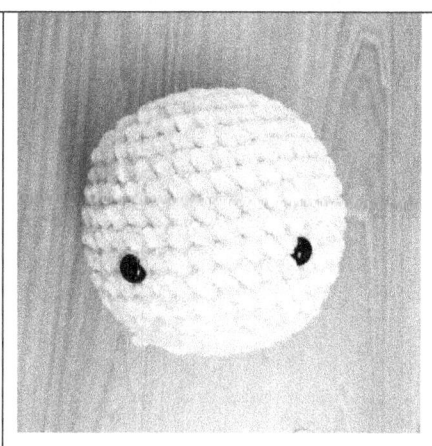

Limbs

Start with Pink Yarn

With the head facing downwards, working in front loops of Round 15, insert the crochet to the first stitch and take the pink yarn, start crocheting:

17ch, starting in the 3rd ch from hook, crochet along the chain: 15dc, skip 2st on the rnd 15, slst *(we have done the first limb)*, slst on the working round.

Continue repeat this process untill you have total of 8 limbs.

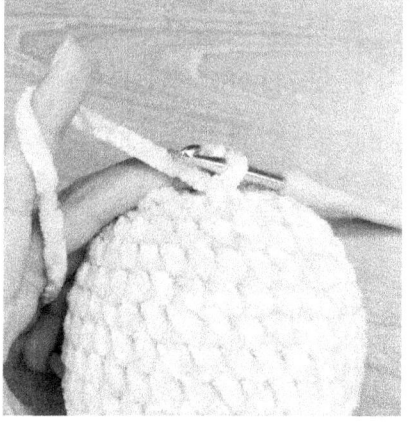

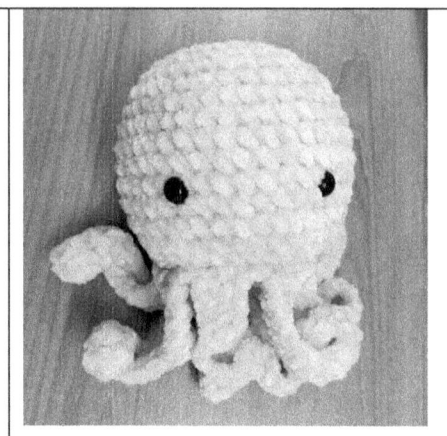

Dots

Start with Light Pink Yarn

- **1st dot**: 5sc into MR [5]

  Fasten off, leaving a long tail for sewing.

- **2nd dot**: 7sc into MR [7]

  Fasten off, leaving a long tail for sewing.

- **3rd dot**: 8sc into MR [8]

  Fasten off, leaving a long tail for sewing.

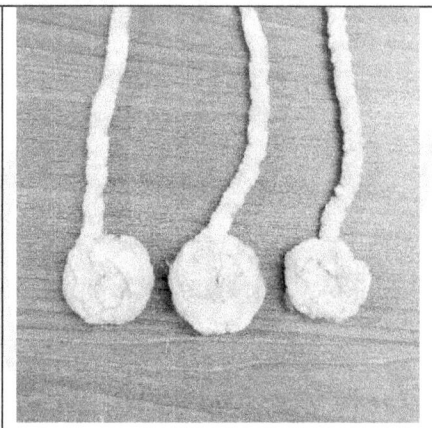

Assembly

- Sew the dots on the head.
- Using black thread, embroider the eyes, eyebrows etc. to create the emotion for octopus.

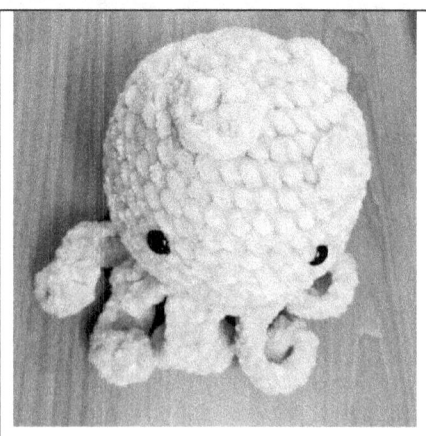

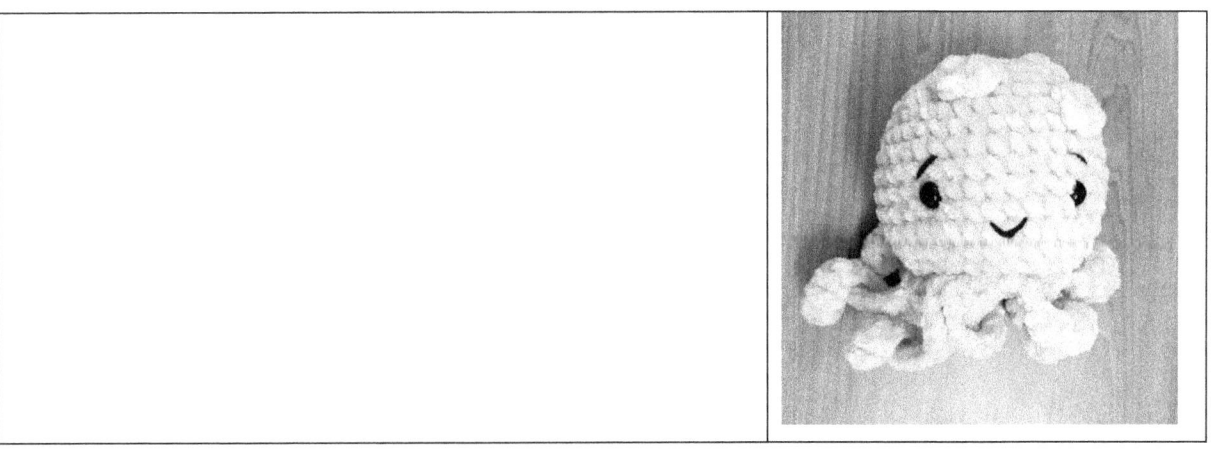

2.3 Shark Crochet Pattern

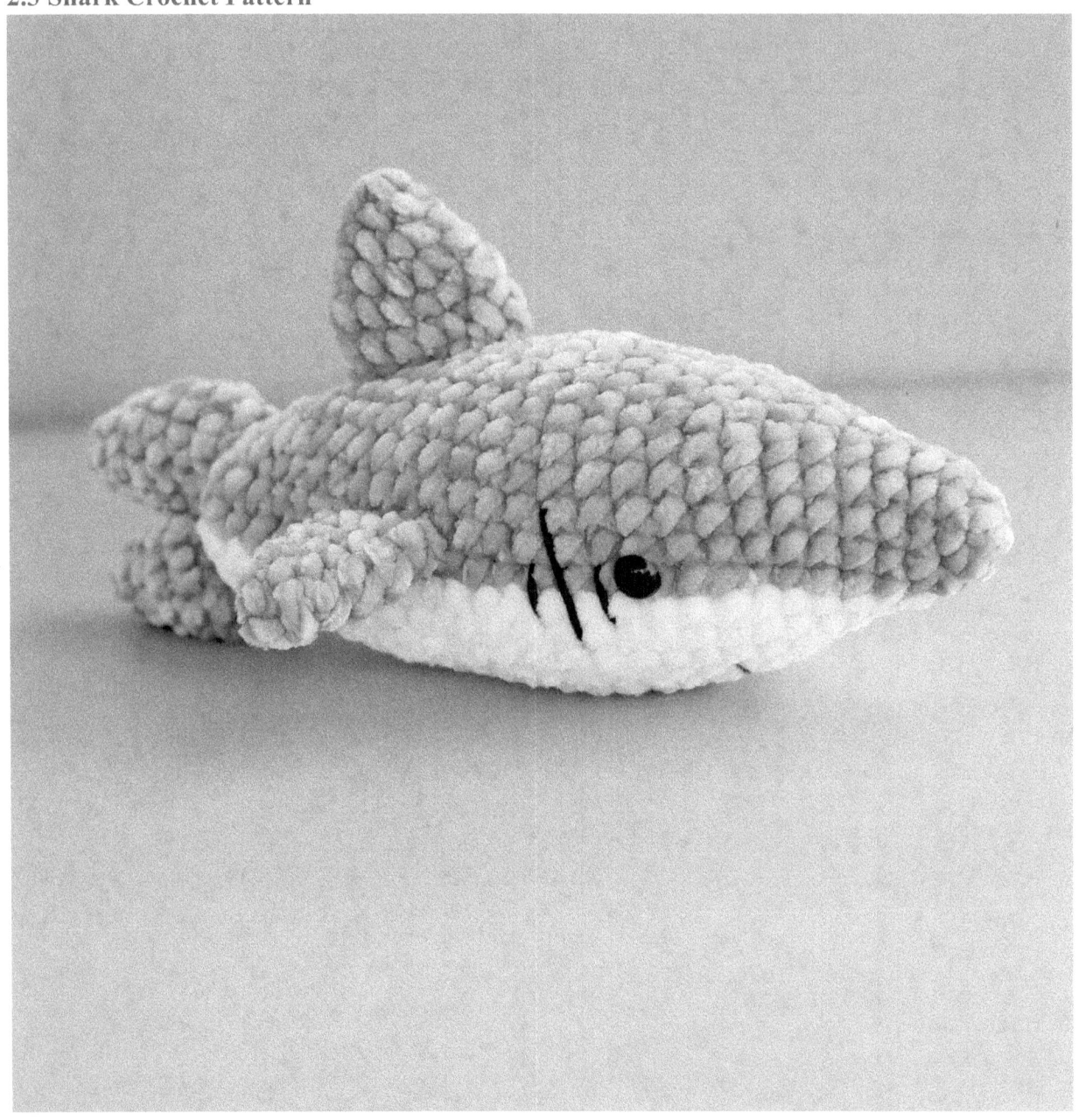

Start with Blue yarn

Rnd 1: 6sc into MR [6]

Rnd 2: (sc, inc) repeat 3 times [9]

Rnd 3: (2sc, inc) repeat 3 times [12]

Add white yarn and do not cut the

Rnd 4:

Now add white yarn (w), do not cut the blue yarn (b)

Rnd 4: w – 3sc, b – inc, 3sc, inc, 3sc, 1sc, w – 1sc into the same st. [15]

Rnd 5: w - 4sc, b – inc, 4sc, inc, 4sc, w – inc [18]

Rnd 6: w – 5sc, b – inc, 5sc, inc, 4sc, w – 1 sc, inc [21]

Rnd 7: w – 6sc, b – inc, 6sc, inc, 4sc, w – 2sc, inc [24]

Rnd 8: w – 7sc, b – inc, 7sc, inc, 4sc, w – 3sc, inc [27]

Rnd 9: w – 7sc, b – 15sc, w – 5sc [27]

Rnd 10: w – 8sc, b – inc, 8sc, inc, 4sc, w – 4sc, inc [30]

Rnd 11: w – 8sc, b – 16sc, w – 6sc [30]

Rnd 12: w – 9sc, b – inc, 9sc, inc, 4sc, w – 4sc, inc [33]

Rnd 13: w – 9sc, b – 17sc, w – 7sc [33]

Rnd 14: w – 9sc, b – 17sc, w – 7sc [33]

Insert the eyes between rounds 10 and 11 on the sides

Rnd 15: w – w5sc, dec, 2sc, b – 9sc, dec, 6sc, w – 3sc, dec, 2sc [30]

Rnd 16: w – 8sc, b – 16sc, w – 6sc [30]

Rnd 17: w – 4sc, dec, 2sc, b – 8sc, dec, 6sc, w – 2sc, dec, 2sc [27]

Rnd 18: w – 7sc, b – 15sc, w – 5sc [27]

Rnd 19: w – 3sc, dec, 2sc, b – 7sc, dec, 6sc, w – 2sc, dec, 1sc [24]

Rnd 20: w – 6sc, b – 14sc, w – 4sc [24]

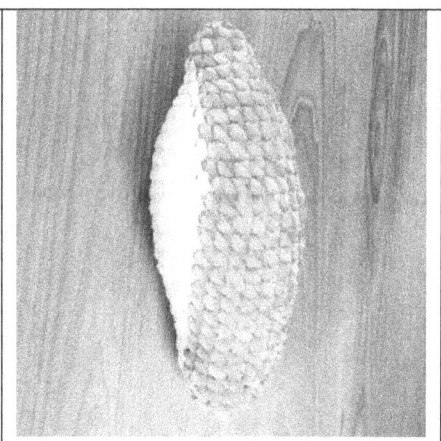

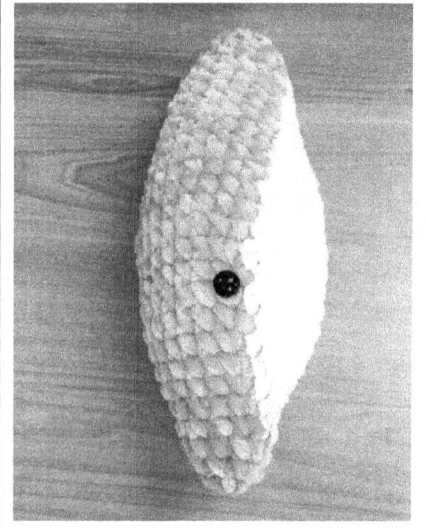

Start stuffing.

Rnd 21: w – 2sc, dec, 2sc, b – 6sc, dec, 6sc, w – 1sc, dec, 1sc [21]

Rnd 22: w – 5sc, b – 13sc, w – 3sc [21]

Rnd 23: w – 1sc, dec, 2sc, b – 5sc, dec, 6sc, w – dec, 1sc [18]

Rnd 24: w – 4sc, b – 12sc, w – 2sc [18]

Rnd 25: w – dec, 2sc, b – [3sc, dec] *2 times, 2sc, w – 2sc [15]

Rnd 26: w – 3sc, b – 10sc, w – 2sc [15]

Rnd 27: w – dec, 1sc, b – 2sc, dec, 3sc, dec, 1sc, w – 2sc [12]

Rnd 28: w – dec, b – [2sc, dec] *2 times, w – 2sc [9]

Stuff to the end.
Cut the white yarn and weave in the ends. Cut the blue yarn and sew the opening with it, weave in the ends.

Side Fins (make 2)

Start with Blue Yarn

Rnd 1: 4sc into MR [4]

Rnd 2: (sc, inc) repeat 2 times [6]

Rnd 3: (1sc, inc) repeat 3 times [9]

Rnd 4: 8sc, inc [10]

Rnd 5 – Rnd 6: 10sc all around – total 2 rounds [10]

Do not stuff. Leave a long tail for sewing.
Fold and edges together and sew them.

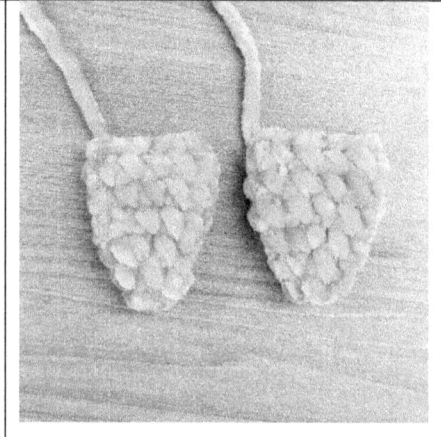

Tail Fins (make 2)

Start with Blue Yarn

Rnd 1: 4sc into MR [4]

Rnd 2: (sc, inc) repeat 2 times [6]

Rnd 3: (sc, inc) repeat 3 times [9]

Rnd 4: (sc, inc) repeat 2 times, 5sc [11]

Rnd 5: 11sc all around [11]

Rnd 6: 6sc, dec, 3sc [10]

Rnd 7: 5sc (uncomplete round)

Do not stuff. Leave a thread for sewing

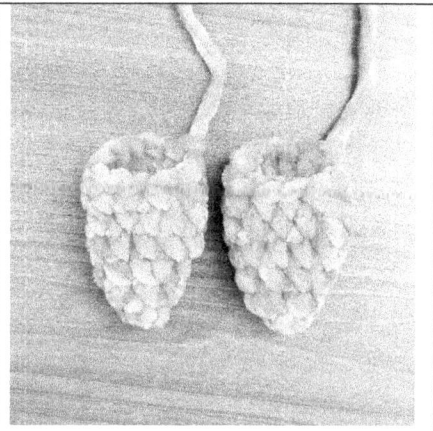

Upper Fin

Start with Blue Yarn

Rnd 1: 4sc in the magic ring [4]

Rnd 2: (sc, inc) repeat 2 times [6]

Rnd 3: (sc, inc) repeat 3 times [9]

Rnd 4: (2sc, inc) repeat 3 times [12]

Rnd 5: 12sc [12]

Rnd 6: 4sc, 4hdc, 4sc [12]

Do not stuff. Leave a thread for sewing.

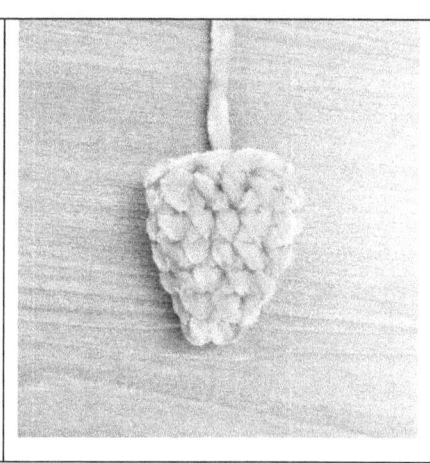

1. Sew tail fins on the back
2. Sew the side fins on rounds 16-19 around the color change line
3. Sew the upper fins on rounds 16-20
4. Use black yarn to embroider a smile on 10-11 rounds and 3 stripes on each side in front of the side fins.

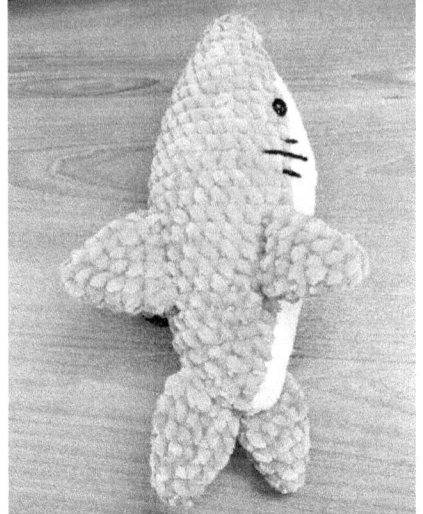

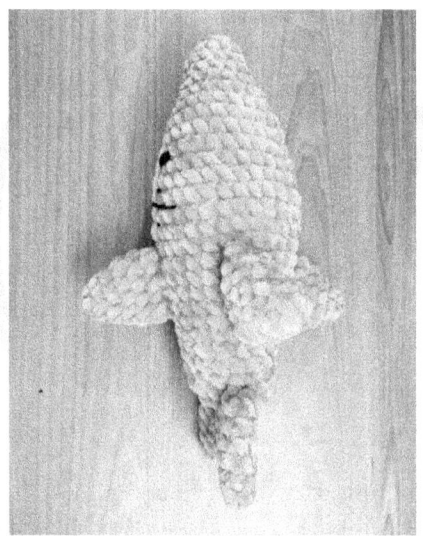

2.4 Seahorse

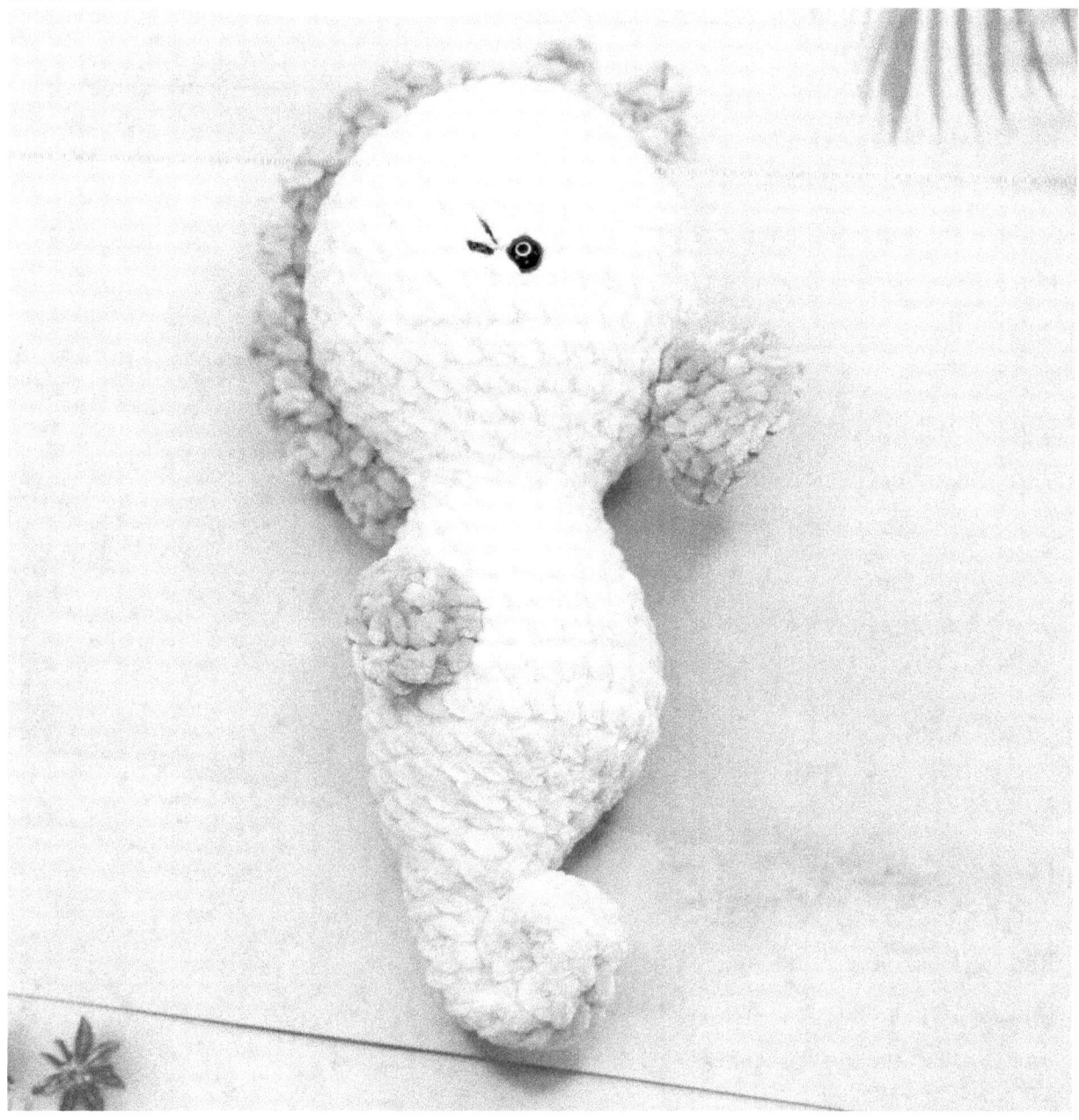

HEAD

Start with Yellow Yarn

Rnd 1: 6sc into MR [6]

Rnd 2: 6inc [12]

Rnd 3: (sc, inc) repeat 6 times [18]

Rnd 4: (2sc, inc) repeat 6 times [24]

Rnd 5: (3sc, inc) repeat 6 times [30]

Rnd 6: (4sc, inc) repeat 6 times [36]

Rnd 7: (5sc, inc) repeat 6 times [42]

Rnd 8 – Rnd 12: 42sc around – total 5 rounds [42]

Rnd 13: (5sc, dec) repeat 6 times [36]

Rnd 14: (4sc, dec) repeat 6 times [30]

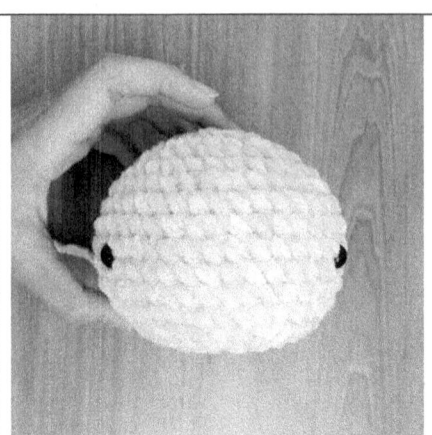

Insert the eyes between R10 and R11 with 14st apart)

Rnd 15: (3sc, dec) repeat 6 times [24]

Rnd 16: (2sc, dec) repeat 6 times [18]

Stuff

Rnd 17: (sc, dec) repeat 6 times [12]

Rnd 18: 12sc [12]

Rnd 19: (3sc, inc) repeat 3 times [15]

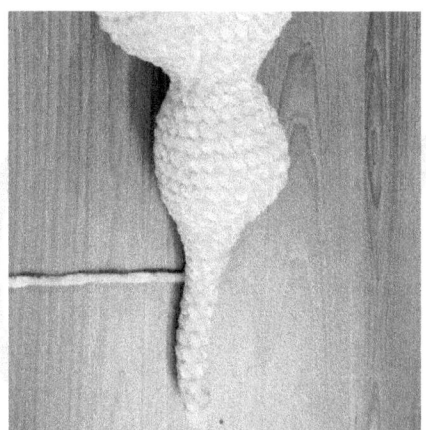

Rnd 20: (4sc, inc) repeat 3 times [18]

Rnd 21: (4sc, inc) repeat 3 times [21]

Rnd 22: (6sc, inc) repeat 3 times [24]

Rnd 23: (7sc, inc) repeat 3 times [27]

Rnd 24:(8sc, inc) repeat 3 times [30]

Rnd 25: 30sc around [30]

Rnd 26: 30sc around [30]

Rnd 27: 6sc, (sc, dec) repeat 6 times, 6sc [24]

Rnd 28: 6sc, (sc, dec) repeat 4 times, 6sc [20]

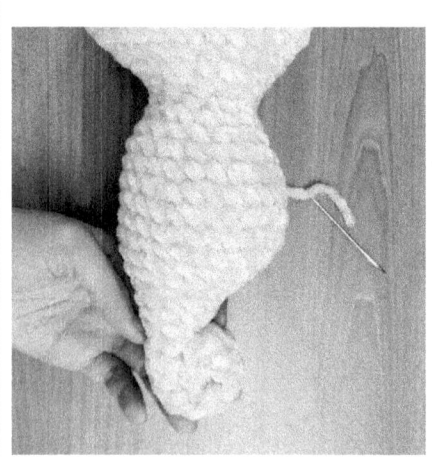

Rnd 29: 4sc, (sc, dec) repeat 4 times, 4sc [16]

Rnd 30: 2sc, (sc, dec) repeat 4 times, 2sc [12]

Rnd 31: 12sc [12]

Stuff

Rnd 32: 5sc, dec, 5sc [11]

Rnd 33: 4sc, dec, 5sc [10]

Rnd 34: 4sc, dec, 4sc [9]

Rnd 35: 3sc, dec, 4sc [8]

Rnd 36: 3sc, dec, 3sc [7]

Rnd 37 – Rnd 44: 7sc

Close and cut the yarn, leaving a long tail for sewing.

Roll up the tail and secure with a yarn tail.

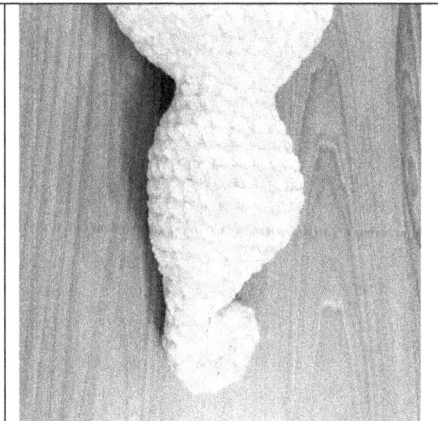

Coronet

Start with Blue Yarn

Make a foundation chain of 28ch, start from 4th ch from hook, crochet along the chain

Rnd 1: slst, (sc, 3chain picot, slst) repeat ( ) 12 times

Close and cut the yarn, leaving a long tail for sewing.

Scan for Picot St

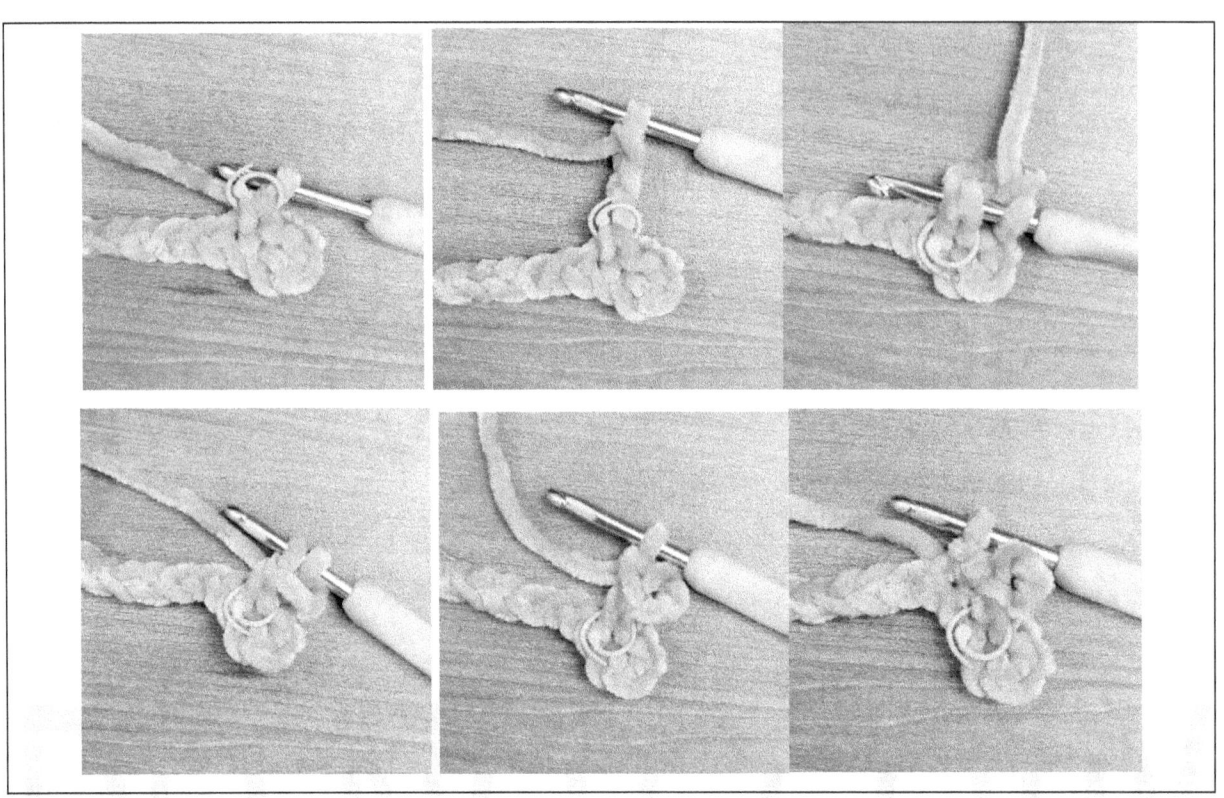

FINS (make 2)
Start with Blue Yarn

Make ch3, start in 3rd ch from the hook, crochet: 3dc, ch1,

turn, 2sc in each stitch [6]

Close and cut the yarn, leaving a long tail for sewing.

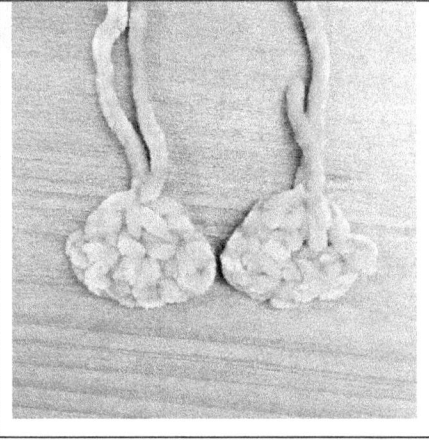

Snout	
Start with Blue Yarn	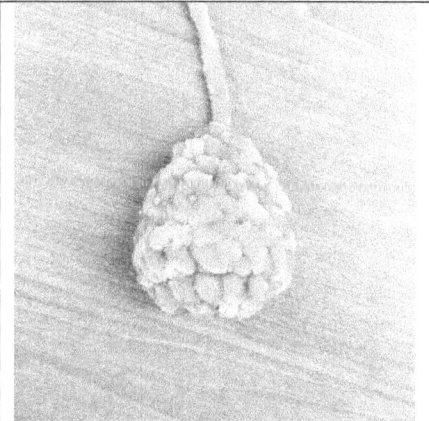
Rnd 1: 6sc into MR	
Rnd 2: 6inc [12]	
Rnd 3: (sc, inc) repeat 6 times [18]	
Rnd 4: BLO all (4sc, dec) repeat 3 times [15]	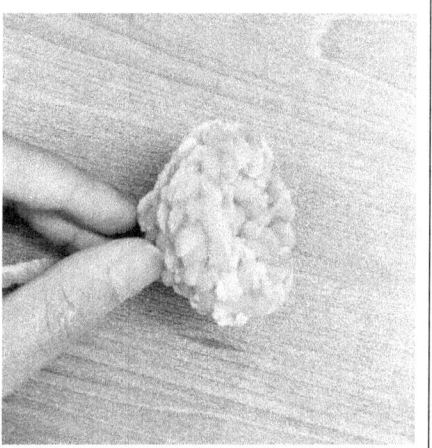
R5: (3sc, dec) repeat 3 times [12]	
R6: (2sc, dec) repeat 3 times [9]	
R7: (sc, dec) repeat 3 times [6]	
Fasten off and leave a long tail to sew	
*Instead of stuffing the snout, I push the base inside (**see photos**)*	

Assembly	
<ul><li>Sew the fins in place</li><li>Sew the snout on to the face</li><li>Sew the coronet in place on top of the head</li></ul>	

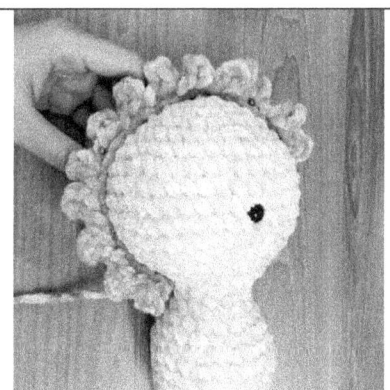 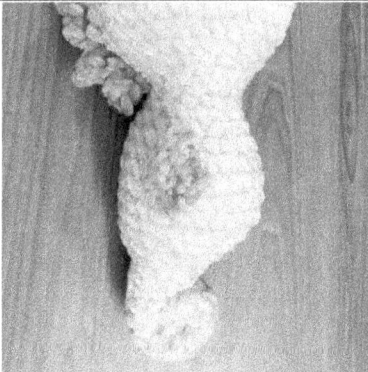 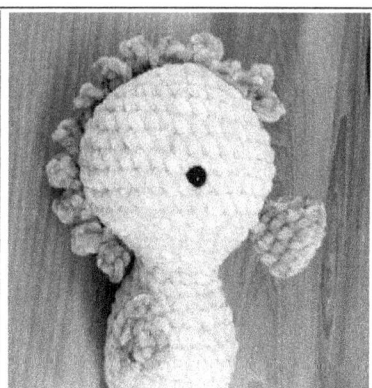

2.5 Whale Crochet Pattern

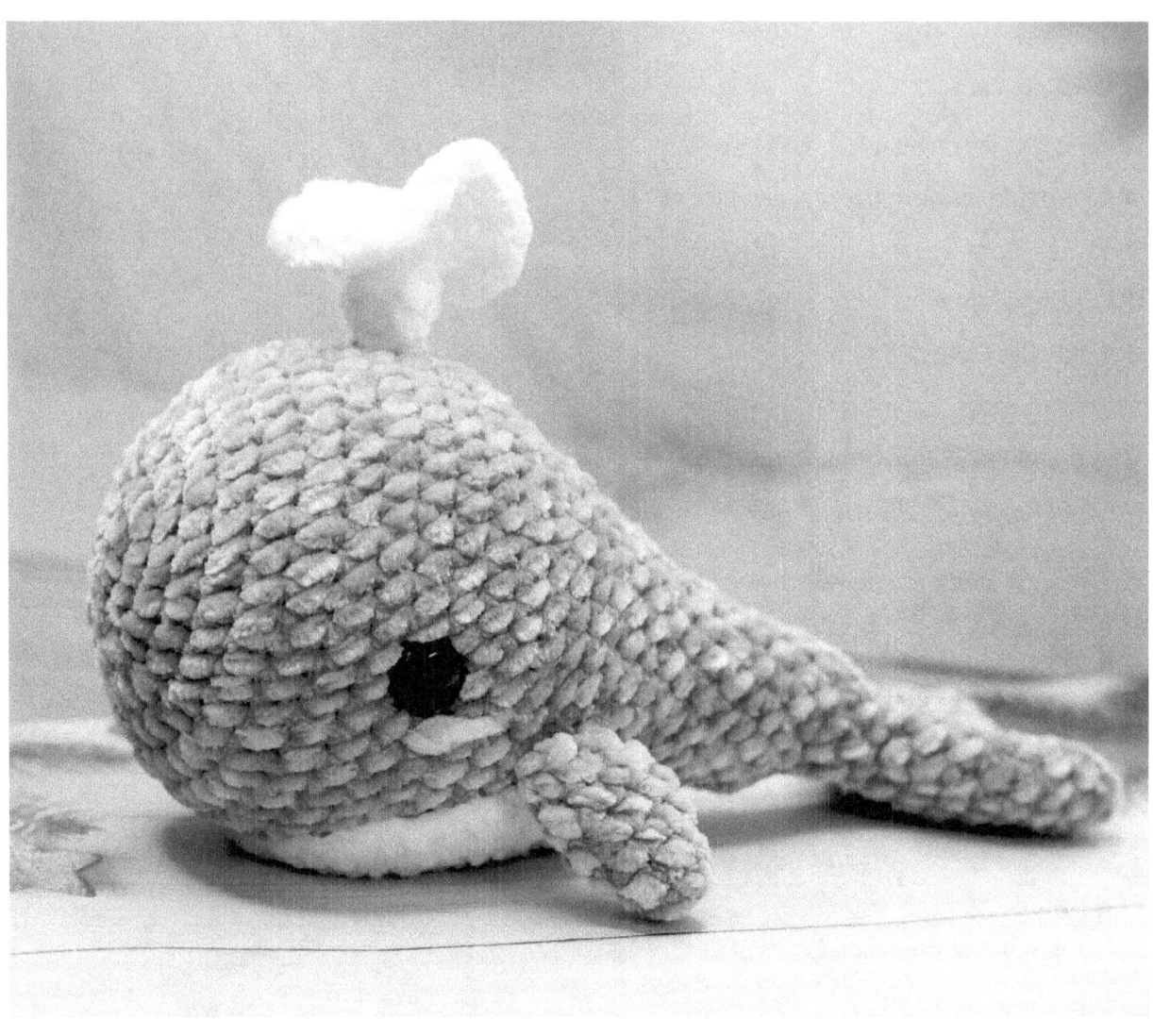

Body

Start with Blue Yarn

Rnd 1: 8sc in the MR [8]

Rnd 2: 8inc [16]

Rnd 3: (sc, inc) repeat 8 times [24]

Rnd 4: (2sc, inc) repeat 8 times [32]

Rnd 5: (3sc, inc) repeat 8 times [40]

Rnd 6: (4sc, inc) repeat 8 times [48]

Rnd 7 – Rnd 12: 48sc around [48]

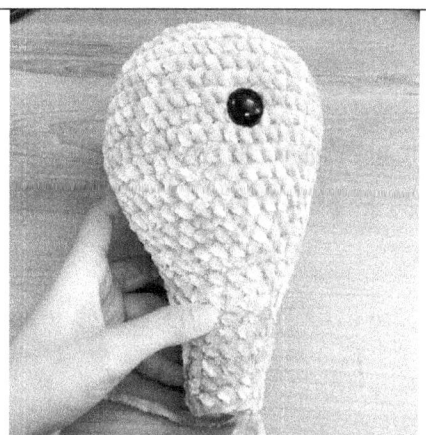

Rnd 13: 14sc, (3sc, dec) 4 times, 14sc [44]

Rnd 14: (4sc, dec) repeat 2 times, (2sc, dec) repeat 5 times, (4sc, dec) repeat 2 times [35]

Rnd 30:

Rnd 15 – Rnd 16: 35sc around- total 2 rounds [35]

Rnd 17: (3s, dec) repeat 2 times, (2sc, dec) repeat 4 times, (sc, dec), 4sc [28]

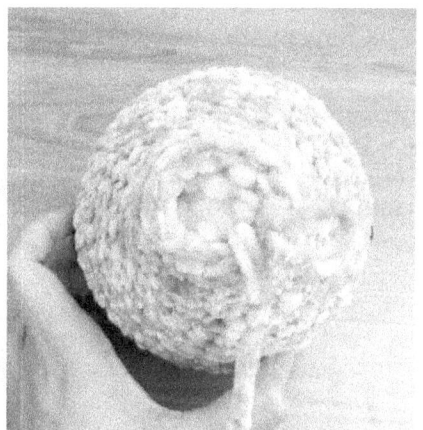

Rnd 18 – Rnd 19: 28sc around [28]

Rnd 20: (2sc, dec) repeat 2 times, (sc, dec) repeat 5 times, (2sc, dec), sc [20]

Rnd 21 – Rnd 22: 20sc around – total 2 rounds [20]

Insert the eyes between rounds 10 and 11 on the side of the head. Stuff.

Rnd 23: 2dec, 12sc, 2dec [16]

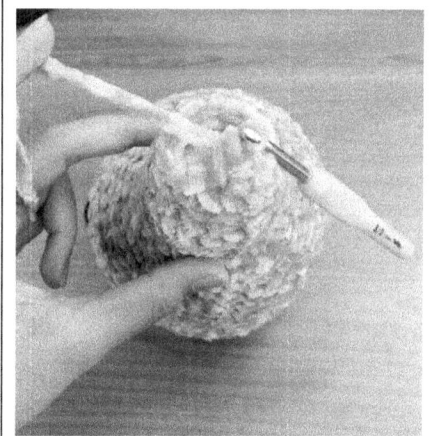

Rnd 24-26: sc around [16]

Rnd 27: 3dec, 8sc, dec [12]

Rnd 28-29: sc around [12]

Stuff.

Rnd 30: *Make sc until you reach the center of the round, in line with the top of the head* (about 2 sts)

Split the round so there are 6 stitches on each side: 6sc [6]

Rnd 31: (sc, inc) repeat 3 times [9]

Rnd 32: (2sc, inc) repeat 3 times [12]

Rnd 33 – Rnd 36: 12sc around – total 4 rounds [12]

Rnd 37: (2sc, dec) repeat 3 times [9]

Rnd 38: (sc, dec) repeat 3 times [6]

Close and cut the yarn. There is one fin completed.

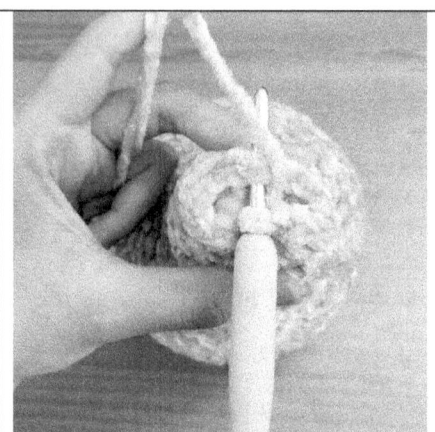

Start the second fin. *Insert Blue yarn into one of the stitches along the side for the new fin. Do the exact same thing we did with the first fin:*

Rnd 30: 6sc [6]

Rnd 31: (sc, inc) repeat 3 times [9]

Rnd 32: (2sc, inc) repeat 3 times [12]

Rnd 33 – Rnd 36: 12sc around – total 4 rounds [12]

Rnd 37: (2sc, dec) repeat 3 times [9]

Rnd 38: (sc, dec) repeat 3 times [6]

Close and cut off the yarn. Leave a long tail for sewing. Close up the hole between two fins.

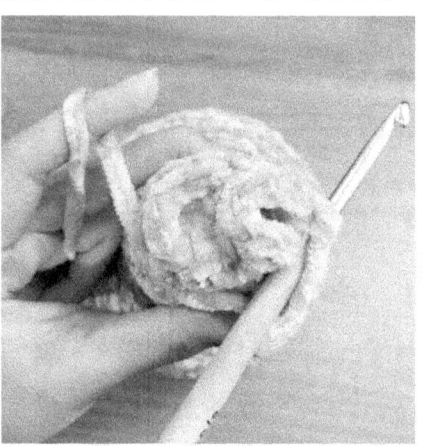

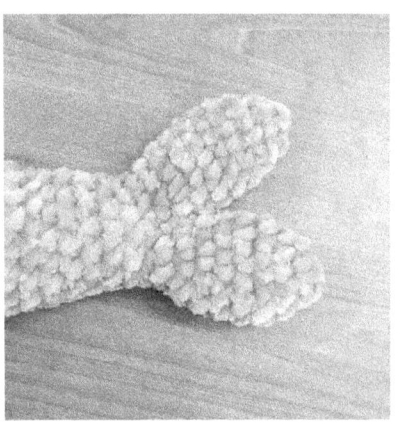

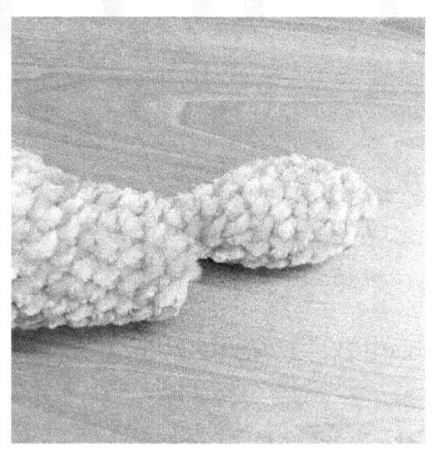

Chest Plate (make 2)

Start with White Yarn

Rnd 1: 8sc in to the MR [8]

Rnd 2: 8inc [16]

Rnd 3: (sc, inc) repeat 8 times [24]

Rnd 4: (2sc, inc) repeat 8 times [32]

Rnd 5: (3sc, inc) repeat 8 times [40]

Rnd 6: (4sc, inc) repeat 8 times [48]

Rnd 7: 48sc around [48]

Cut off the yarn and leave a long tail for sewing.

Attach chest plate to rounds Rnd 9 – Rnd 22 of the bottoms of the whale. Mark your position with fabric pins. Leave about 3-5 stitches of space from each eye.

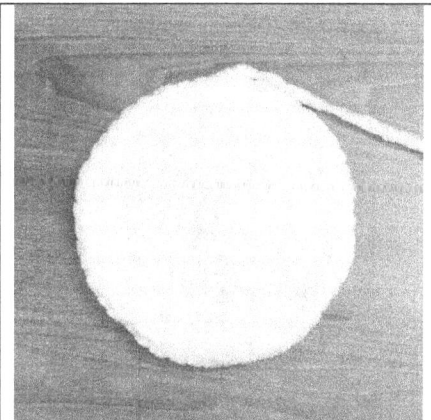

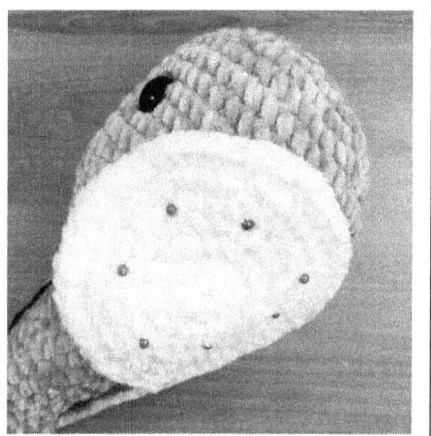

Side Fins (make 2)

Start with Blue Yarn

Rnd 1: 6sc in the magic ring [6]

Rnd 2: 6sc around [6]

Rnd 3: (sc, inc) repeat 3 times [9]

Rnd 4 – Rnd 5: 9sc around [9]

Rnd 6: (sc, dec) repeat 3 times [6]

Close and cut off the yarn. Leave a long tail to sew.

Attach fins to Rnd 13 – Rnd 15 beside the chest plate.

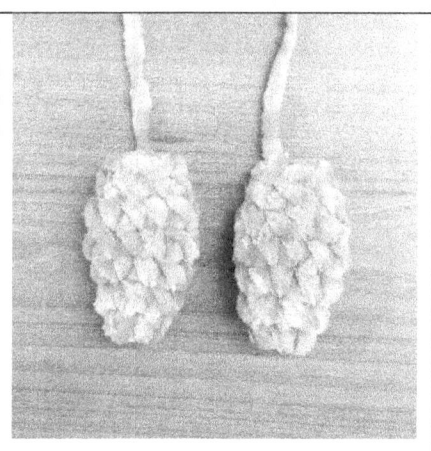

Water Spout	
Start with White Yarn Rnd 1: Make a chain of ch6, join to first chain with a slst [6] Rnd 2 – Rnd 4: 6sc around – total 3 rounds [6] Rnd 5: 6inc [12] Rnd 6: 12inc [24] Rnd 7: 24inc [48] ***Cut off and leave a long tail for sewing.***	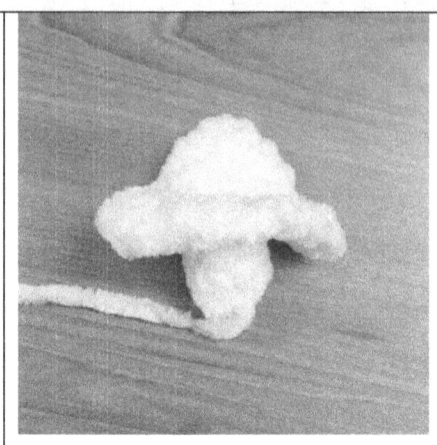

Assembly

- Attach chest plate to rounds 9-22 of the bottoms of the whale. Mark your position with fabric pins. Leave about 3-5 stitches of space from each eye.
- Attach fins to rounds 13-15 beside the chest plate.
- Attach spout on rounds 9-11 on the top of the head.

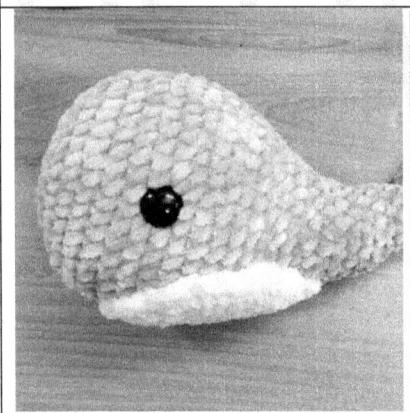 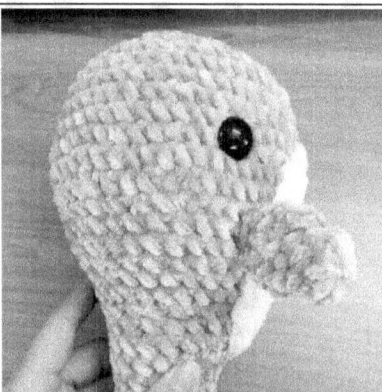 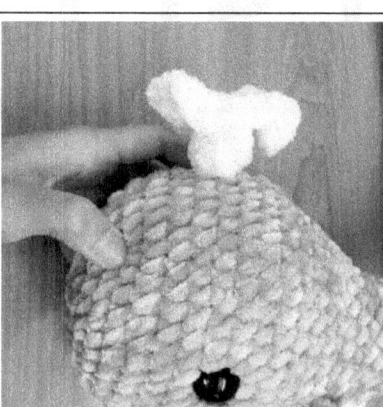

2.6 Sunflower Turtle

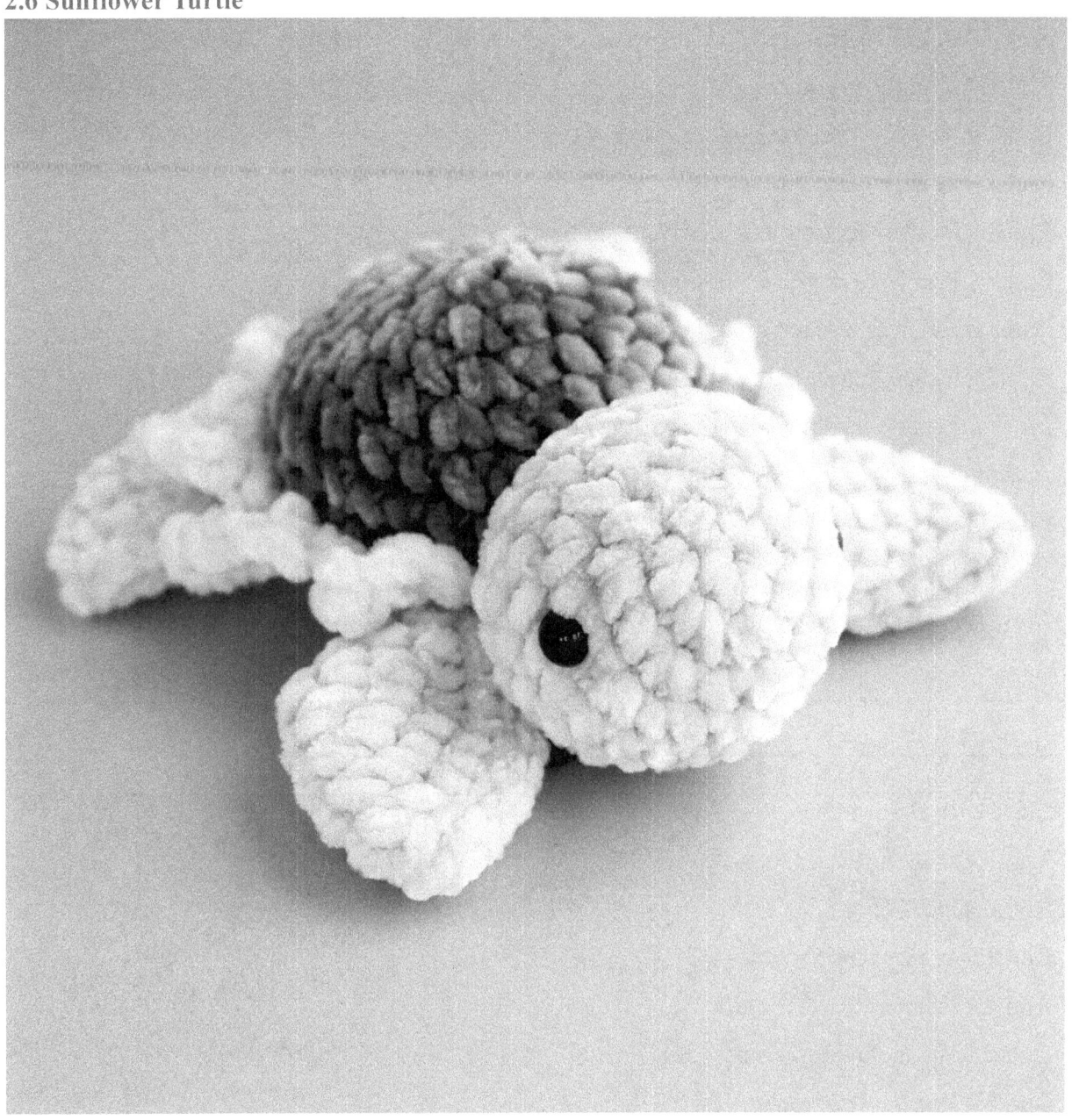

Head

Start with Skin Yarn

Rnd 1: 6sc in the magic ring [6]

Rnd 2: 6inc [12]

Rnd 3: (sc, inc) repeat 6 times [18]

Rnd 4: (2sc, inc) repeat 6 times [24]

Rnd 5 – Rnd 7: 24sc around – total 3 rounds [24]

Rnd 8: (2sc, dec) repeat 6 times [18]

Rnd 9: (sc, dec) repeat 6 times [12]

Insert the eyes between rounds 4 and 5 (8 sts apart). Start stuffing.

Rnd 10: 6dec [6]

Stuff to the end.

Close the opening and cut off the yarn. Leave a long tail to sew.

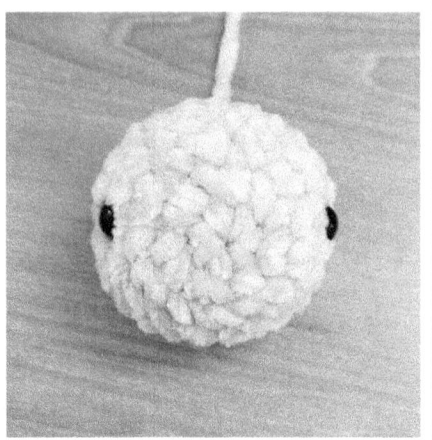

Body

Start with Brown Yarn

Rnd 1: 6sc in the magic ring [6]

Rnd 2: 6inc [12]

Rnd 3: (sc, inc) repeat 6 times [18]

Rnd 4: (2sc, inc) repeat 6 times [24]

Rnd 5: (3sc, inc) repeat 6 times [30]

Rnd 6 – Rnd 7: 30sc around – total 3 rounds [30]

Rnd 8: BLO all 30sc around [30]

Rnd 9: (3sc, dec) repeat 6 times [24]

Rnd 10: (2sc, dec) repeat 6 times [18]

Rnd 11: (sc, dec) repeat 6 times [12]

Rnd 12: 6dec [6]

Close the opening and cut off the yarn.

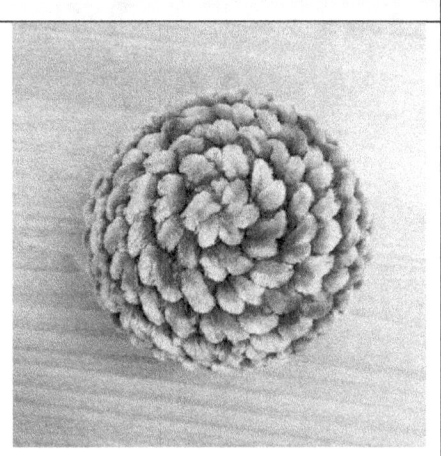

Join the Yellow yarn in any stitch and start crochet:

Rnd 1: slst in next 2sts, **[(slst on the next st + ch2 + dc all into the same stitch where slst is worked + ch2 picot), (dc + ch2 + slst all into on the next stitch)]**. Repeat [ ] 7 more times (petals), slst on next 2 stitches.

Fasten off.

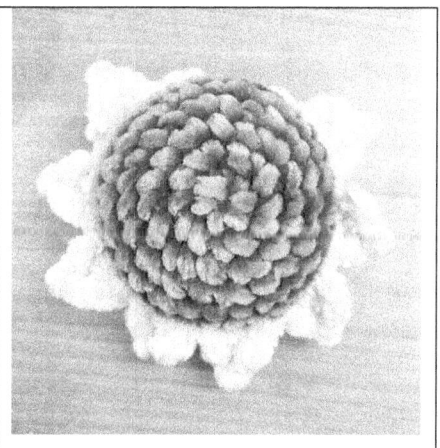

Front flippers (make 2)

Start with Skin Yarn

Rnd 1: 6sc in the magic ring [6]

Rnd 2: 6inc [12]

Rnd 3: (sc, inc) repeat 6 times [18]

Rnd 4: (2sc, inc) repeat 6 times [24]

Rnd 5: 24sc around [24]

Fold and edges together and sew them. Cut off and leave a long tail to sew.

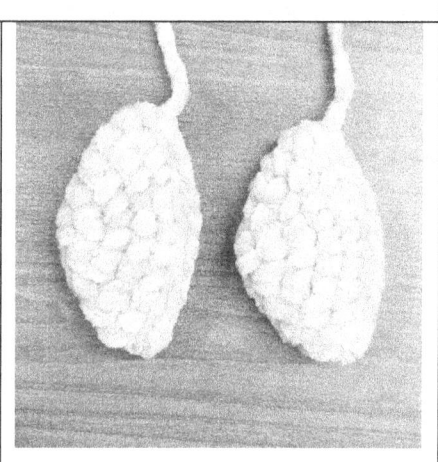

Behind Flippers (make 2)

Start with Skin Yarn

Rnd 1: 6sc in the magic ring [6]

Rnd 2: 6inc [12]

Rnd 3: (sc, inc) repeat 6 times [18]

Rnd 4: 18sc around [18]

Fold and edges together and sew them. Cut off and leave a long tail to sew.

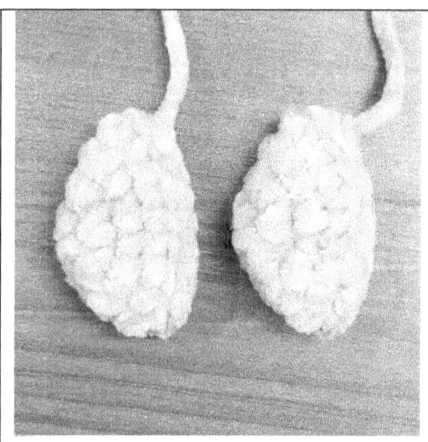

Assembly

1. Sew the head to the body

2. Sew the flippers to the body.

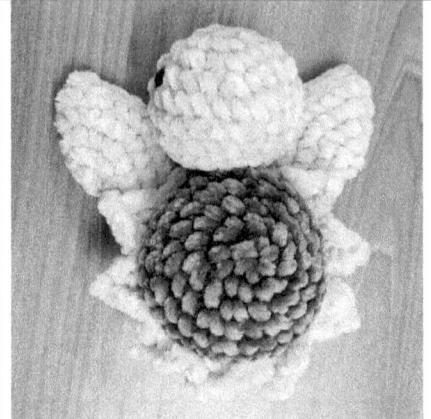

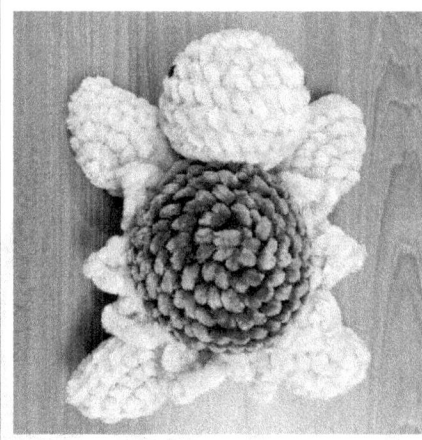

2.7 Starfish

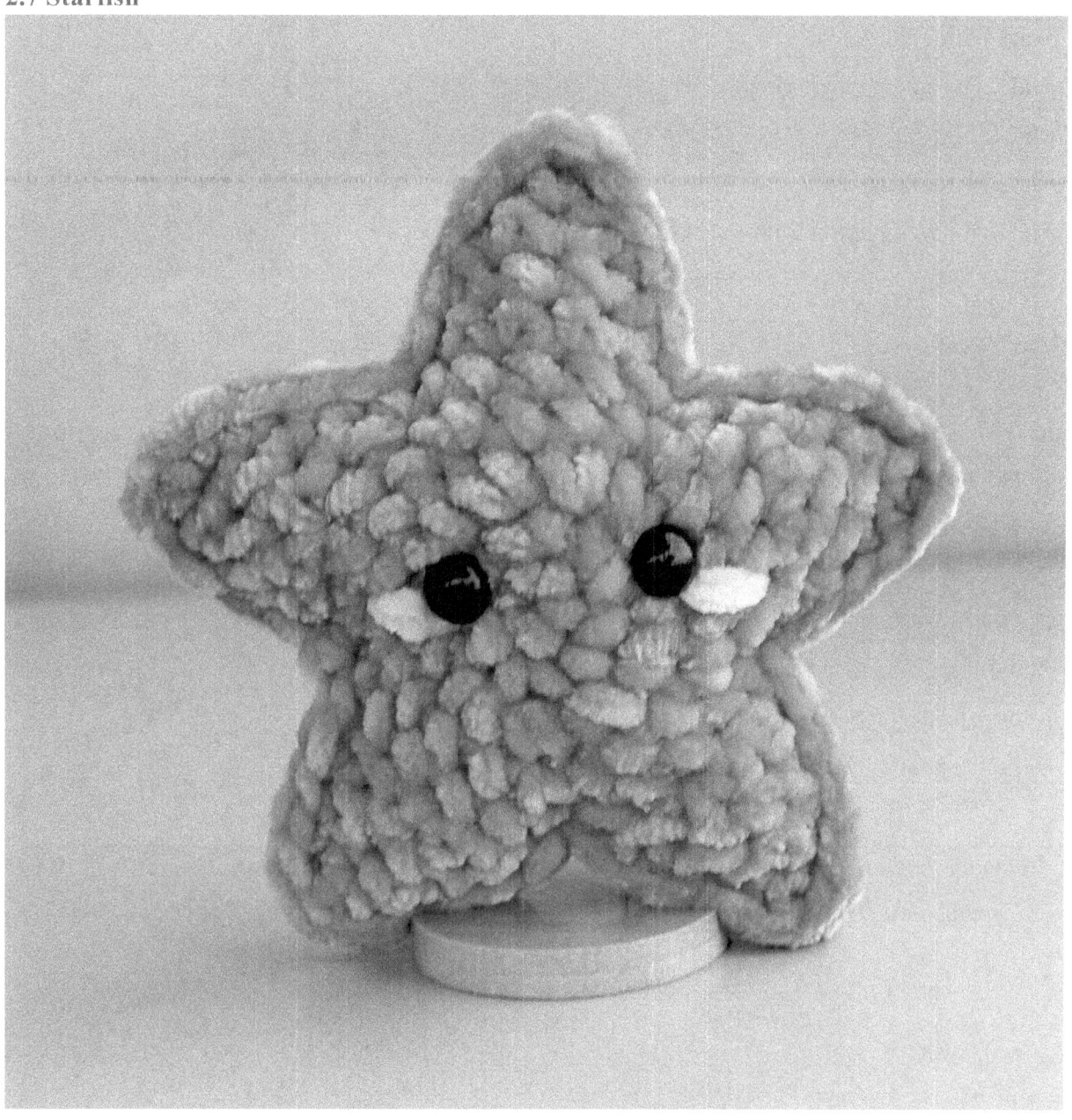

Start with Pink Yarn

Rnd 1: 5sc in the magic ring [5]

Rnd 2: 5inc [10]

Rnd 3: 10inc [20]

Rnd 4: (3sc inc) repeat 5 times [25]

Do not cut the yarn, start crocheting rays of starfish

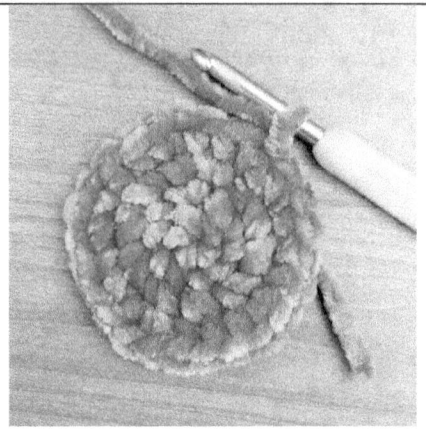

1st ray of star:

Rnd 1: 5sc, 1ch turn [5]

Rnd 2: 3sc, dec, 1ch turn [4]

Rnd 3: 2sc, dec, 1ch turn [3]

Rnd 4: sc, dec, 1ch turn [2]

Rnd 5: dec [1].

Cut off the yarn.

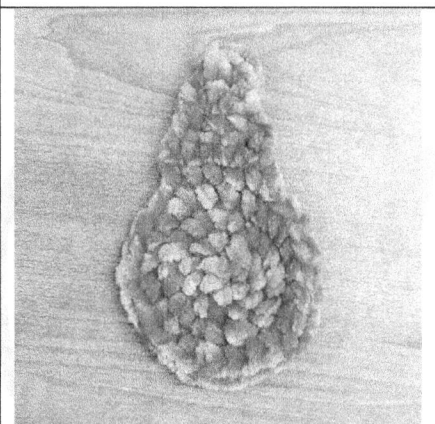

Attach the thread to the next loop and in the same way crochet the next ray of the star.

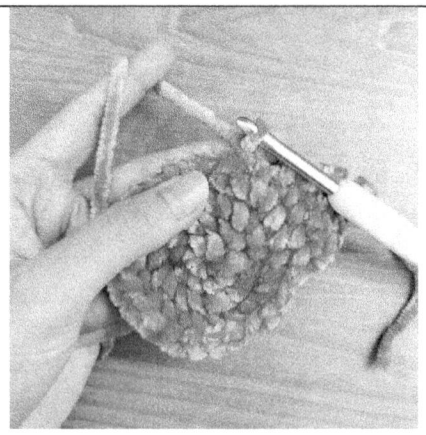

Stuff.

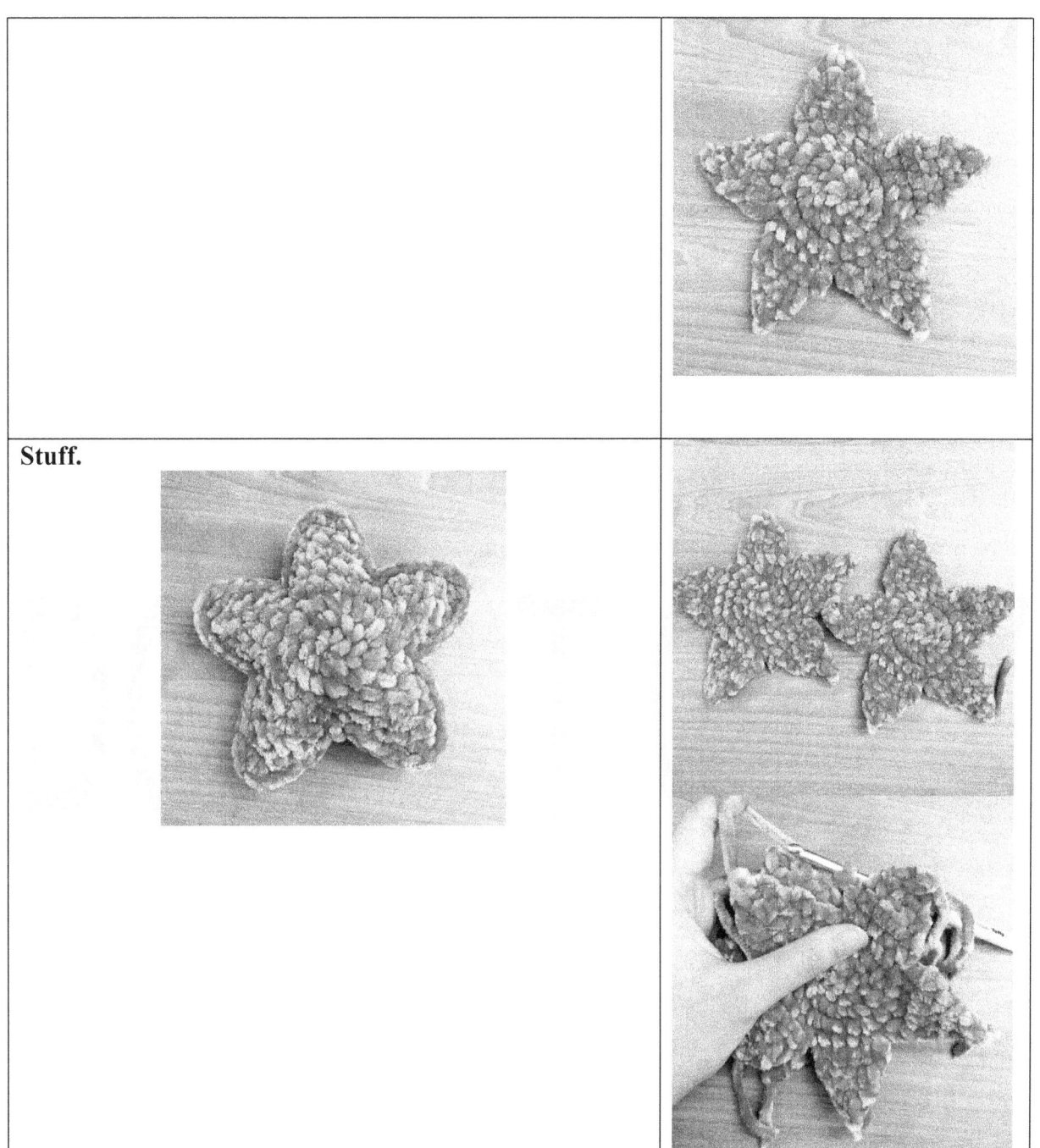

2nd part of star

Do the same with 1st part.	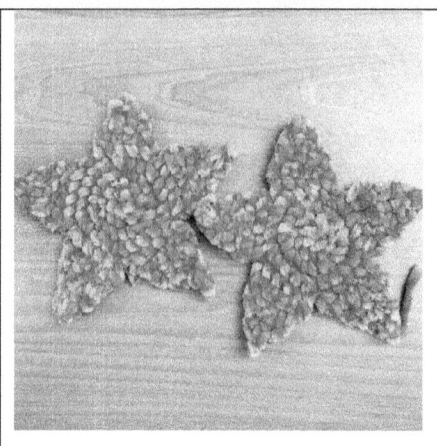

Assembly

• Attach two parts to each other and crochet along the edge with sc. • Stuff	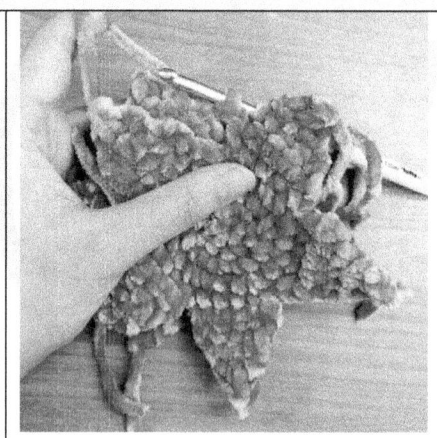
• Insert the eyes between rounds 3 and 4	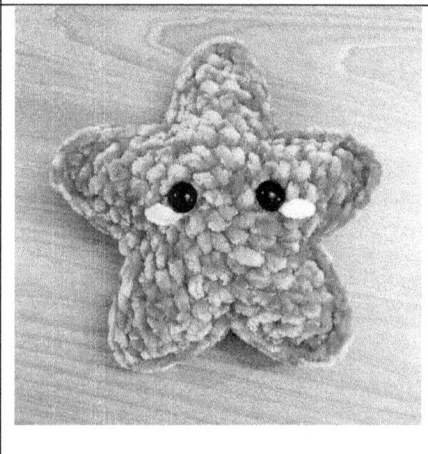

2.8 Axolotl

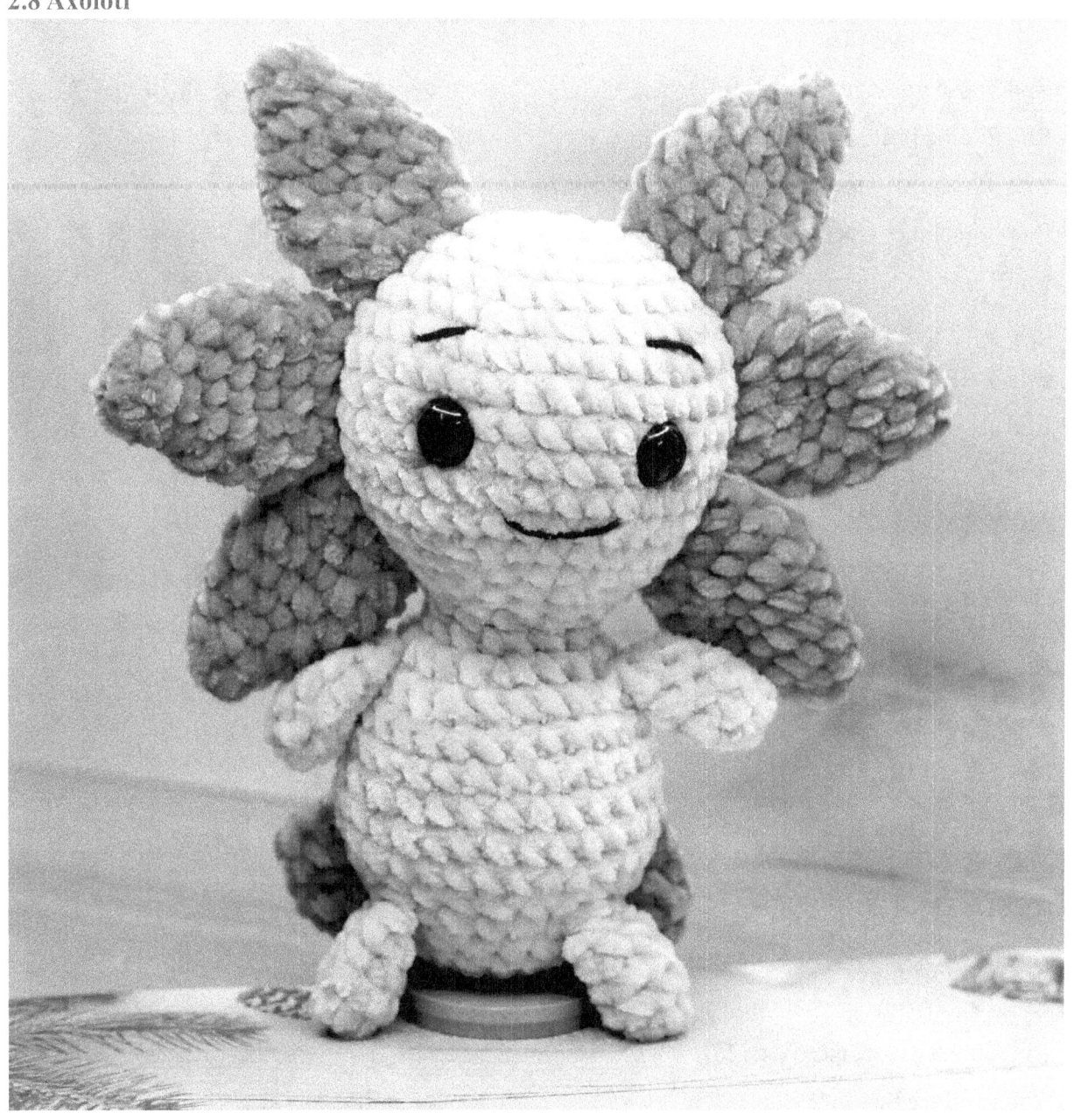

Head

Use Light Pink Yarn

Rnd 1: 6sc in the magic ring [6]

Rnd 2: 6inc [12]

Rnd 3: (sc, inc) repeat 6 times [18]

Rnd 4: (sc, inc) repeat 6 times [24]

Rnd 5: (3sc, inc) repeat 6 times [30]

Rnd 6: (4sc, inc) repeat 6 times [36]

Rnd 7 – Rnd 12: 36sc around [36]

Rnd 13: (4sc, dec) repeat 6 times [30]

Rnd 14: (3sc, dec) repeat 6 times [24]

Insert the eyes between rounds 9 and 10 with 6 sts apart

Rnd 15: (2sc, dec) repeat 6 times [18]

Rnd 16: (sc, dec) repeat 6 times [12]

Stuff the head. Don't cut off the yarn and continue to the body.

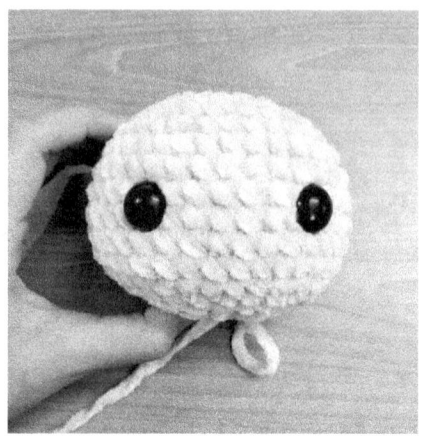

Body

Rnd 17: 12sc [12]

Rnd 18: (sc, inc) repeat 6 times [18]

Rnd 19: (2sc, inc) repeat 6 times [24]

Rnd 20: inc, 11sc, inc, 11sc [26]

Rnd 21: 25sc, inc [27]

Rnd 22: inc, 26sc [28]

Rnd 23: 13sc, inc, 13sc, inc [30]

Rnd 24 – Rnd 25: 30sc around [30]

Rnd 25: (3sc, dec) repeat 6 times [24]

Rnd 26: 24sc around [24]

Rnd 27: (2sc, dec) repeat 6 times [18]

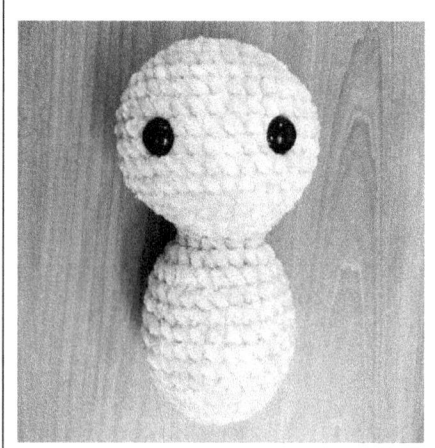

Rnd 28: 18sc around [18]

Rnd 29: (sc, dec) repeat 6 times [12]

Stuff.

Rnd 30: 6dec [6]

Fasten off and cut off the yarn.

Leg (make 4)

Start with Light Pink Yarn

Rnd 1: 6sc in the magic ring [6]

Rnd 2 – Rnd 4: 6sc around – total 3 rounds [6]

Fold in half and crochet through 2 opposite stitch with 2sc [2].

Fasten off. Do not stuff. Leave a long tail to sew.

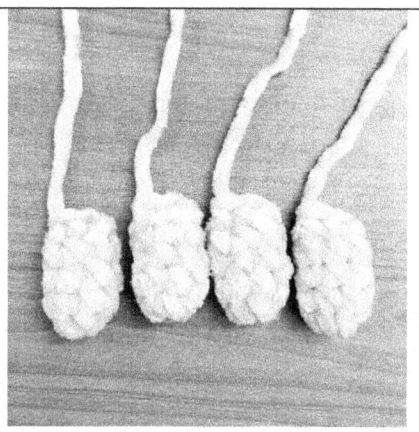

ANTENNAE (make 6)

Start with Dark Pink Yarn

Rnd 1: 6sc into the magic ring [6]

Rnd 2: 6sc around [6]

Rnd 3: 6inc [12]

Rnd 4 – Rnd 5: 12sc around – total 2 rounds [12]

Rnd 6: (2sc, dec) repeat 3 times [9]

Rnd 7: (sc, dec) repeat 3 times [6]

Fasten off. Leave a long tail to sew.

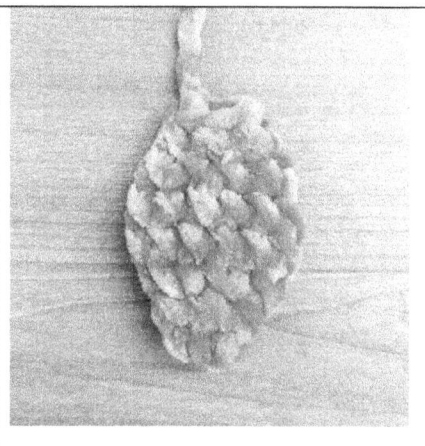

Tail

Start with Dark Pink Yarn

We will use the surface crochet technique here.

Start crochet from the right side at Round 10 of the body, go over to the bottom, then go to the left side of the body, and end at Rnd 10.

Rnd 1: **[(sc + hdc into same stich), 2dc inc, (hdc + sc into the same stitch), slst]**

Repeat [ ] two more times

Fasten off and hide the yarn tail.

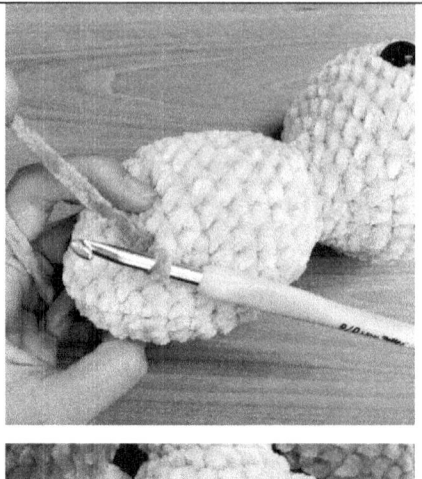

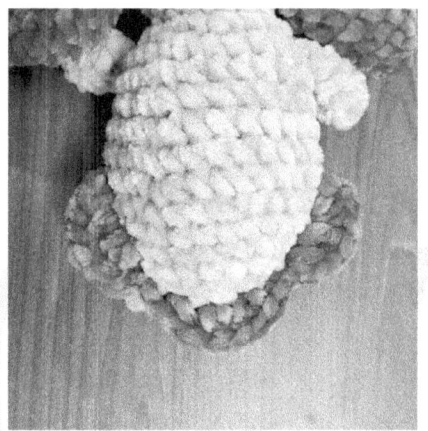

Assembly

- Use crochet thread to embroider the face as the photo.
- Sew the antennae to the head: 2 first ones are opposite across MR, then sew others next to the first one.
- Sew 4 legs to the body.

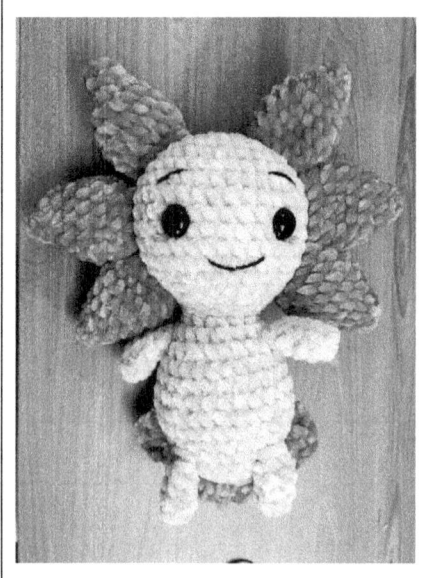

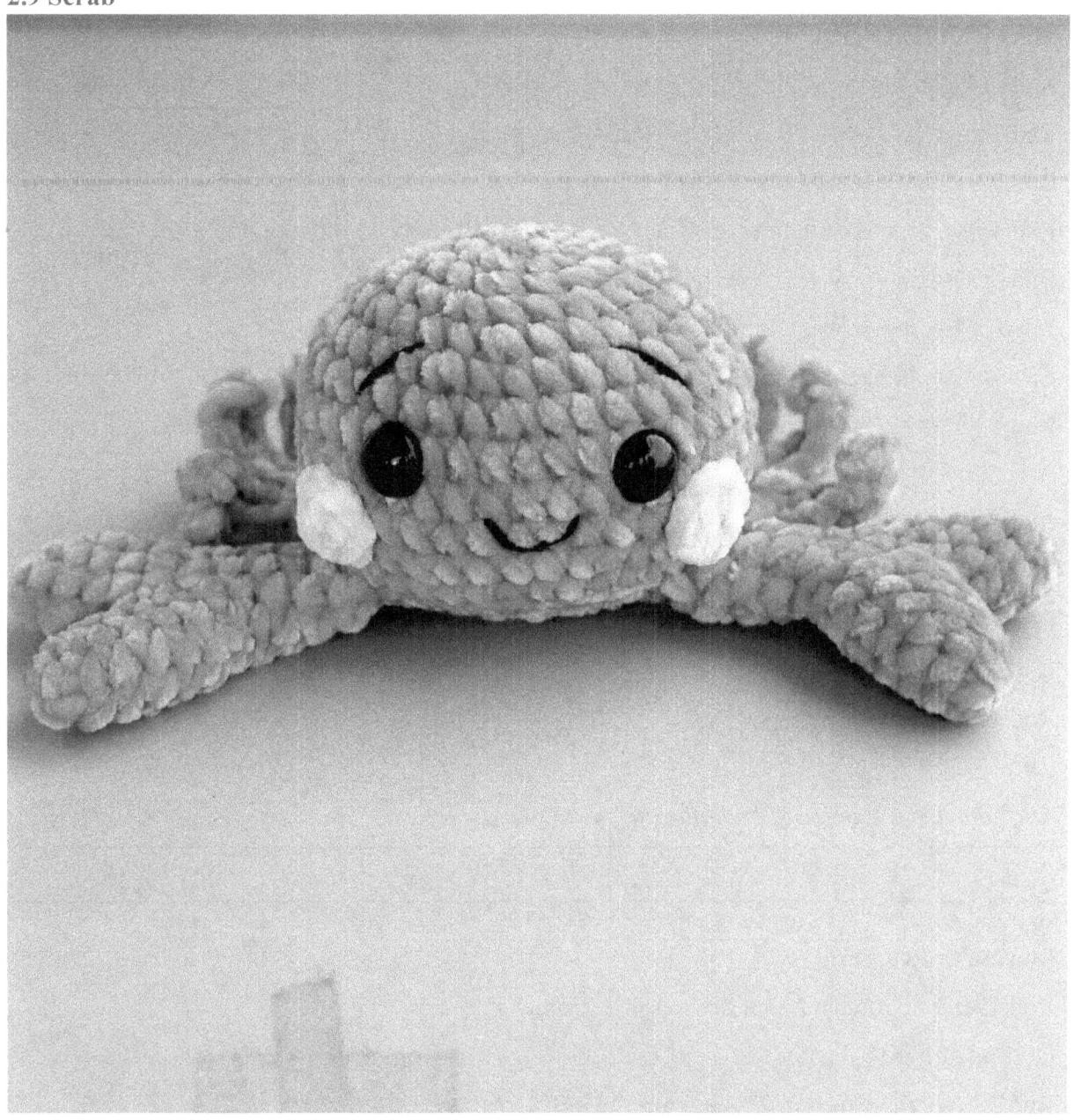

Shell

Start with Red Yarn

Rnd 1: 6sc in the magic ring [6]

Rnd 2: 6inc [12]

Rnd 3: (sc, inc) repeat 6 times [18]

Rnd 4: (sc, inc) repeat 6 times [24]

Rnd 5: (3sc, inc) repeat 6 times [30]

Rnd 6: (4sc, inc) repeat 6 times [36]

Rnd 7: (5sc, inc) repeat 6 times [42]

Rnd 8 – Rnd 12: 42sc around [42]

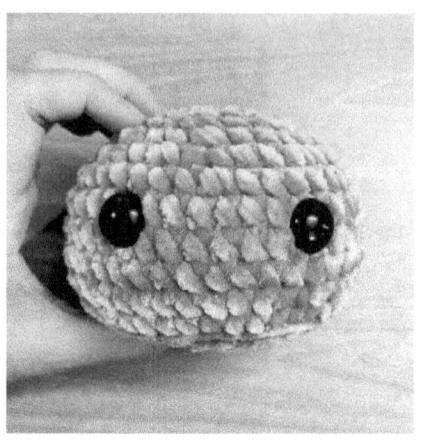

Insert the eyes between rounds 8 and 9 with 7 sts separates

Rnd 13: BLO all (5sc, dec) repeat 6 times [36]

Rnd 14: 18 dec [18]

Rnd 15: 9dec [9]

Rnd 16: sc, 4dec [5]

Stuff the head. Fasten off and hide the yarn tail.

Leg (make 2)

Start with Red Yarn

Rnd 1: ch6, starting in 2nd ch from the hook, crochet: 5sc, ch1 and turn [5]

Rnd 2: **[(sc, ch7, work in 2nd ch from the hook, crochet: 6sc)]. Repeat [ ] 4 times total to make 4 legs.**

Fasten off and leave a long tail to sew.

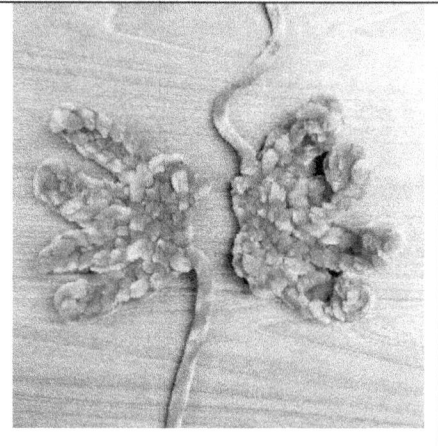

Pincers (make 2)

Start with Red Yarn

You will make 2 points for each pincer and join at round 5.

Rnd 1: 4 sc in the magic ring [4]

Rnd 2: (sc, inc) repeat 2 times [6]

Rnd 3: (2sc, inc) repeat 2 times [8]

Rnd 4: 8sc around [8]

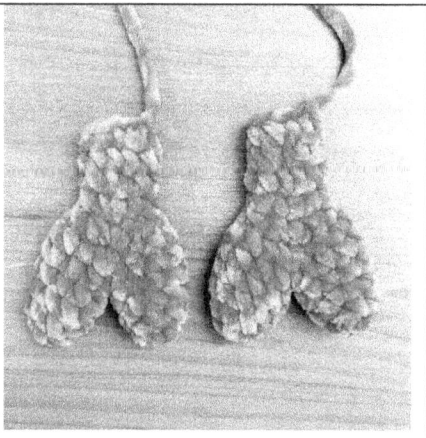

Fasten off the first point, and continue with the second.

Rnd 5: 8sc (then work directly into the 1st point), 8sc [16]

Rnd 6: 16sc around [16]

Rnd 7: 8dec [8]

Rnd 8 – Rnd 11: 8sc around – total 4 rounds [8]

Fasten off. Do not stuff. Leave a long tail to sew.

Cheek (make 2)

Use Pink Yarn

Rnd 1: 6sc in the magic ring [6]

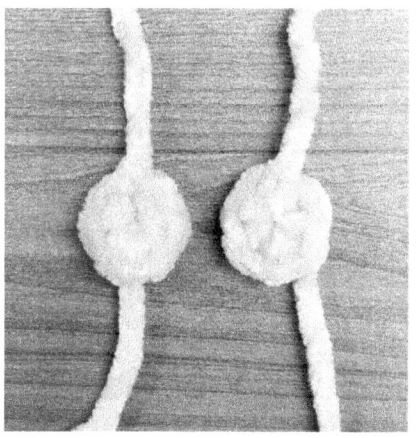

Assembly	
• Sew the pincers and legs to either side of the shell, whip stitching to the front loop left over for round 13. • Using back thread yarn, embroider eyebrows from rounds 6 to 7 of the shell. • Sews the cheeks from rounds 11 to 13.	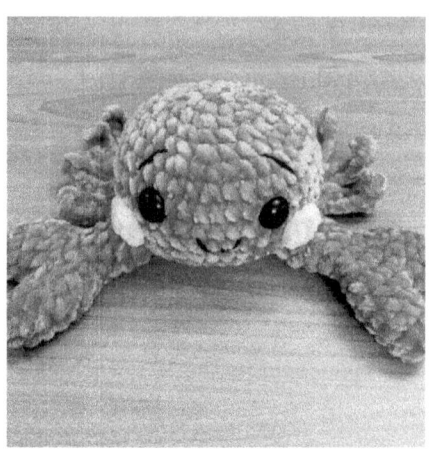

2.10 Seal

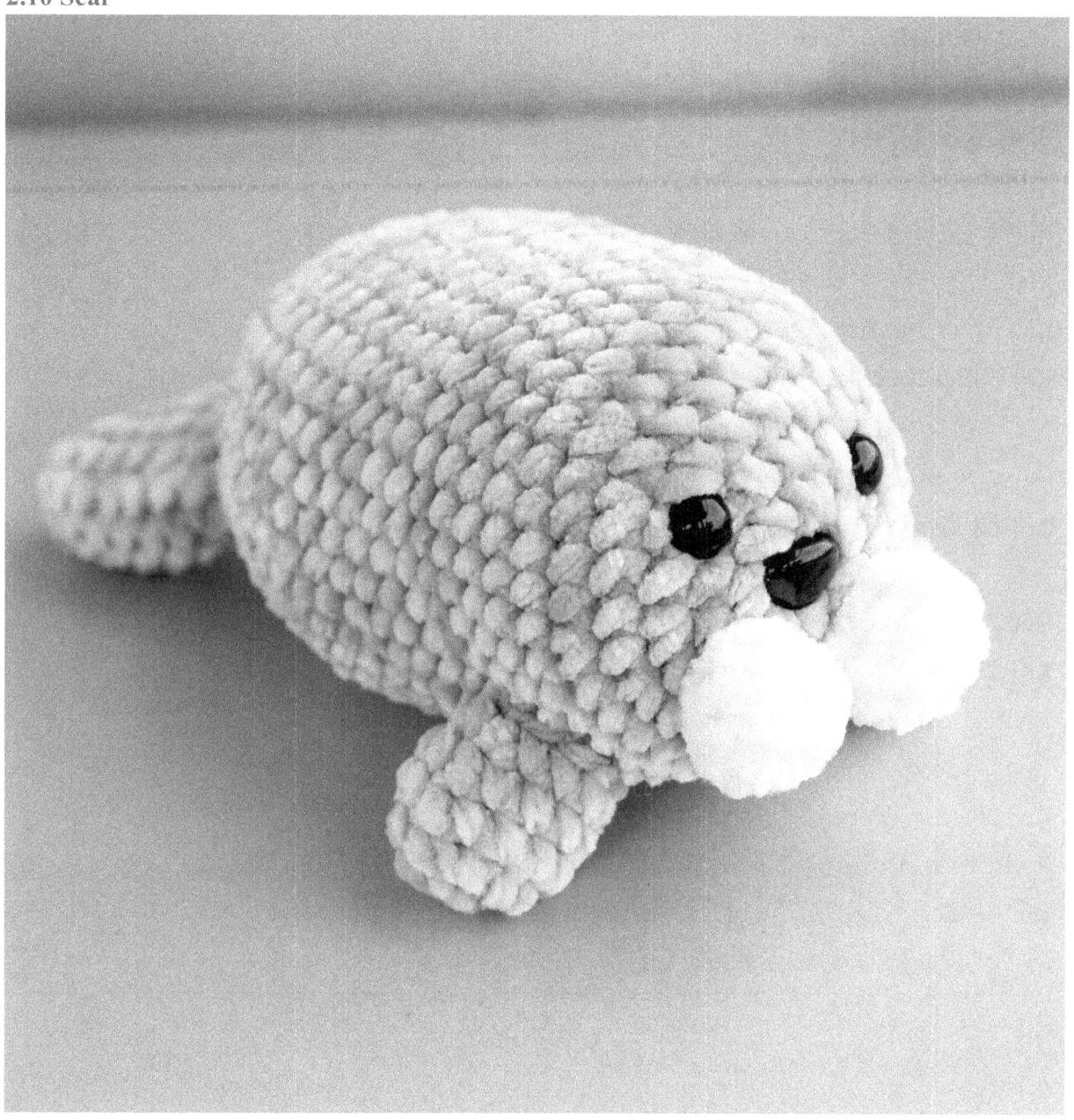

Head and Body

Start with GREY Yarn

Rnd 1: 6sc in the magic ring [6]

Rnd 2: 6inc [12]

Rnd 3: (sc, inc) repeat 6 times [18]

Rnd 4: (sc, inc) repeat 6 times [24]

Rnd 5: (3sc, inc) repeat 6 times [30]

Rnd 6: (4sc, inc) repeat 6 times [36]

Rnd 7 Rnd 20: 36sc around – total 14 rounds [36]

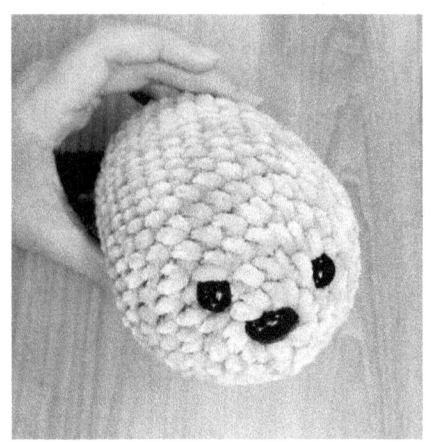

Insert the mouse in the center of magic ring, insert the eyes between rounds 3 and 4 with 5 sts apart

Rnd 21: (4sc, dec) repeat 6 times [30]

Rnd 22 – Rnd 23: 30sc around [30]

Rnd 24: (3sc, dec) repeat 6 times [24]

Rnd 25: 24sc around [24]

Rnd 26: (2sc, dec) repeat 6 times [18]

Rnd 27: (sc, dec) repeat 6 times [12]

Rnd 28: 6dec

Stuff. Fasten off and hide the yarn tail.

Tail (make 2)

Start with Grey Yarn

Rnd 1: 6sc in the magic ring [6]

Rnd 2: (sc, inc) repeat 3 times [9]

Rnd 3: (2sc, inc) repeat 3 times [12]

Rnd 4 – Rnd 8: 12sc around [12]

Rnd 9: 6dec [6]

Fasten off and leave a long tail to sew.

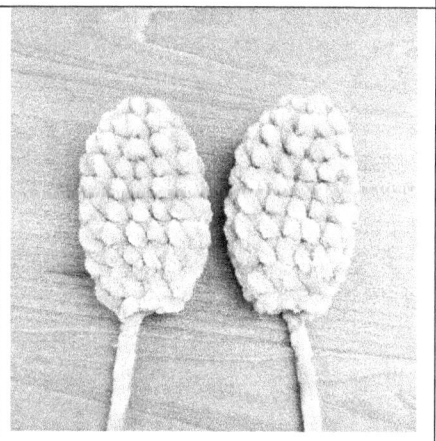

Cheek (make 2)

Start with White Yarn

Rnd 1: 6sc in the magic ring [6]

Rnd 2: (sc, inc) repeat 3 times [9]

Rnd 3 – Rnd 4: 9sc around – total 2 rounds [9]

Fasten off. Do not stuff. Leave a long tail to sew.

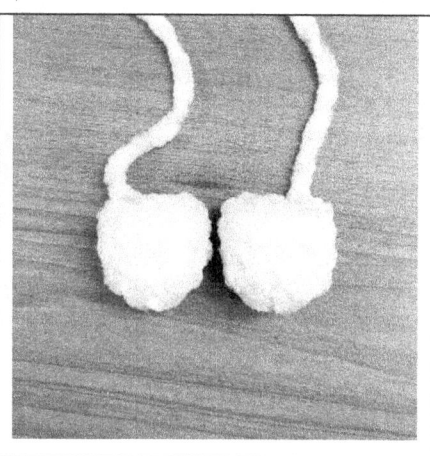

Arms (make 2)

Start with Grey Yarn

Rnd 1: 6sc in the magic ring [6]

Rnd 2: 6inc [12]

Rnd 3 – Rnd 5: 12sc around [12]

Fasten off and leave a long tail to sew.

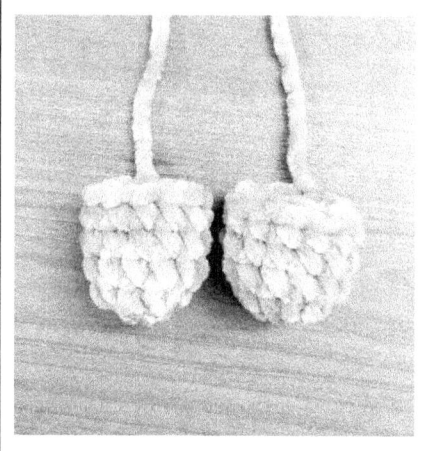

Assembly

- Sew the tails to the end of the body.
- Sew the cheeks to the head, under the eyes
- Sews the arms under the body.

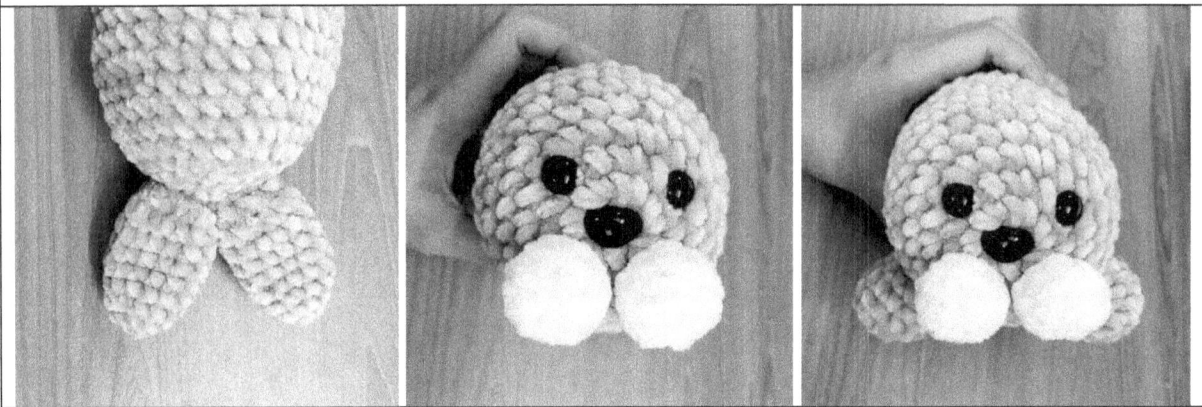

-------------------- **THE END** ------------------------

Any questions, please do not hesitate to contact us via

Email: meesamigu@gmail.com

Instagram: meesamigu